Please return this book to any library in Hackney, on or
before the last date stamped. Fines may be charged if it is late.
Avoid fines by renewing the book (subject to it NOT being reserved).

Call the renewals line on 020 8356 2539

People who are over 60, under 18 or registered disabled
are not charged fines.

G
N
po
A
an
to
m
W
H
th

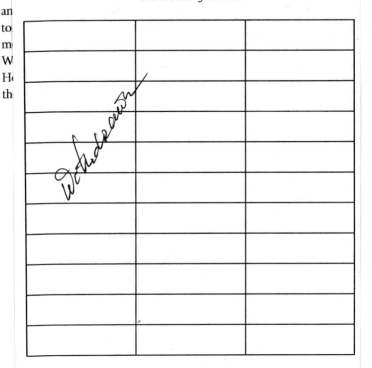

Withdrawn

Hackney

PJ42014

D1341196

9 1300 00017 3462

STRIKE THE CLOUD

Understanding and practising
the teaching of
The Cloud of Unknowing

Graeme Watson

Dedicated to my sister
Katy Haddelsey (1941–2011)

'because she loved greatly'
(*The Cloud of Unknowing*, chapter 16)

First published in Great Britain in 2011

Society for Promoting Christian Knowledge
36 Causton Street
London SW1P 4ST
www.spckpublishing.co.uk

Copyright © Graeme Watson 2011

All rights reserved. No part of this book may be reproduced or transmitted in any
form or by any means, electronic or mechanical, including photocopying,
recording, or by any information storage and retrieval system,
without permission in writing from the publisher.

SPCK does not necessarily endorse the individual views contained
in its publications.

The author and publisher have made every effort to ensure that the external website
and email addresses included in this book are correct and up to date at the time
of going to press. The author and publisher are not responsible for the
content, quality or continuing accessibility of the sites.

Unless otherwise noted, Scripture quotations are taken from the New Revised Standard
Version of the Bible, Anglicized Edition, copyright © 1989, 1995 by the Division
of Christian Education of the National Council of the Churches of Christ
in the USA. Used by permission. All rights reserved.
Extracts from the Authorized Version of the Bible (The King James Bible),
the rights in which are vested in the Crown, are reproduced by permission
of the Crown's Patentee, Cambridge University Press.

British Library Cataloguing-in-Publication Data
A catalogue record for this book is available from the British Library

ISBN 978–0–281–06425–0
eBook ISBN 978–0–281–06647–6

Typeset by Graphicraft Ltd, Hong Kong
Manufacture managed by Jellyfish
First printed in Great Britain by CPI
Subsequently printed in Great Britain by the MPG Books Group

Produced on paper from sustainable forests

Contents

LONDON BOROUGH OF HACKNEY LIBRARY SERVICES			
LOCAT		No. VOLS	
ACC No.			

Foreword

The arrival of Graeme Watson's typescript caused me to turn to my own battered and heavily annotated paperback copy of *The Cloud*, purchased more than forty years ago. The notes made at different times reveal how the fourteenth-century author always has something fresh to impart at whatever stage of spiritual development one may have reached.

One frequently encountered modern difficulty in communicating a living experience of prayer is a confusion of prayer with thinking. 'Whoever hears or reads about all this and thinks that it is fundamentally an activity of the mind [*by travail in their wits*] and proceeds then to work it out along these lines is on quite the wrong track. He manufactures an experience.' Graeme Watson writes with insight about the spiritual truth that God is 'incomprehensible to our intellect but not to our love'.[1]

I very much hope that the practical and contemporary reflections in this book will introduce a new generation of readers to one of the spiritual classics of the English Church, but that reading will soon be replaced by practice. The author of *The Cloud* is aware that clergy in particular read books but the man in the street reads the clergy. That is a salutary truth for all Christians.

Richard Londin:

Acknowledgements

———— ◆•◆•◆ ————

This book could not have been attempted without the help and encouragement of many different people.

First, I am grateful to my tutors on the MA course in Christian Spirituality at Heythrop College, Kensington, Edward Howells and David Lonsdale. They first introduced me to *The Cloud of Unknowing* in 2002, and more recently encouraged me to give a short paper on *The Cloud* at the International Conference on Christian Spirituality at St Mary's College Strawberry Hill, London, in 2009. It was this event that led me to take the plunge in writing this book.

Second, I am grateful to members of the World Community for Christian Meditation, especially those with whom I regularly meditate in our own local ecumenical meditation group at St Mary's Stoke Newington, and also those I have met and come to know as friends and fellow-pilgrims at WCCM gatherings, retreats and conferences. Special thanks are due to Dom Laurence Freeman, the Director of WCCM, for his personal interest and encouragement, and to those who have read and offered comments on one or more chapters, especially Sheelah Hidden, Philip Kitchen, Sheelagh Layet and Jacqueline Russell. I am particularly indebted to Olivia Spencer for reading the whole typescript and for her detailed comments on style and content; and to Stefan Reynolds for his willingness to read all the chapters as they appeared, and for his wise insights and detailed knowledge of *The Cloud* and indeed of fourteenth-century English spirituality. I wish also to thank the Revd Cynthia Bourgeault for her generous response to my request for help, and for her comments and corrections of my final chapter, especially the section on Centering Prayer.

As I am no scholar of Middle English, and cannot claim either to have any specialized knowledge of medieval Christian spirituality, I gladly acknowledge the guidance, learning and insights of James Walsh SJ, the editor of *The Cloud of Unknowing* in the Classics of

Western Spirituality series, on whose edition I have greatly relied for its extensive introduction and notes.

I am grateful to Penguin Books Ltd for permission to quote extensively from *The Cloud of Unknowing and Other Works* (London, 2001), and to the editor and translator, A. C. Spearing, whose introduction and notes I have also found particularly useful. I am extremely grateful also to my publisher, who responded so positively to my venture into writing a book, and especially to my editor, Alison Barr, who has been at all times most responsive and helpful in her advice.

Finally, no words of mine could adequately express my heartfelt thanks to my beloved wife Liz, my companion and fellow-pilgrim on the way, for her loving and critical comments, insights and wholehearted support throughout the course of writing. But for all errors of fact or judgement I take complete responsibility.

Introduction

Although I had been an Anglican priest for some 40 years, I had never read *The Cloud of Unknowing* until 2002. And if I had come across it earlier in my life, I suspect I might well have put it aside as a book intended for monks, nuns and hermits with a specialist calling to contemplative prayer, and certainly not for the likes of a busy parish clergyman as I believed myself to be, let alone for ordinary lay people. How wrong I was. It is not an esoteric book at all, but wholly accessible and direct.

What made the difference was that by that time, I had begun to practise a daily discipline of Christian Meditation as taught by the Benedictine monk John Main (1926–82). This contemplative prayer of silence and stillness came to me as a life-giving gift and grace from God, which has brought about a springtime in my spiritual life, as it has done in the lives of thousands of other people. So when I came across *The Cloud* for the first time, and began to read it, I was absolutely bowled over by its message, and the way in which the author was able to explain the discipline of contemplative prayer in simple but appealing language.

This book is intended for those who would appreciate an introduction to, and commentary on, *The Cloud* written in contemporary terms. A wise teacher of prayer said: 'Pray as you can, not as you can't.' In the world of today there is a growing number of people who have found that the prayer of silence and stillness is a form of prayer that suits them, and given sufficient support and encouragement, they find that they can do it. Called variously the prayer of the heart, contemplative prayer or silent meditation, its roots can be traced back to the very beginnings of Christian history, and it is beautifully described in *The Cloud of Unknowing*.

Some people may have heard of such a form of prayer and are wondering whether it might be right for them. Others may have experienced meditation or contemplative prayer in other faith traditions, or in secular forms, but may not yet be aware of what is available within the Christian tradition. This book is for them too, as it is also for those whose spiritual journey has not yet brought them to explore the possibility of such prayer. Last but not least, it is written for spiritual directors and soul friends who would like to know more about contemplative prayer as practised today.

The author

The Cloud of Unknowing has been widely acknowledged to be both a literary and a spiritual gem. It was written in Middle (medieval) English at very much the same time as Chaucer's *Canterbury Tales* and other great English classics of spirituality by authors such as Julian of Norwich, Walter Hilton and Richard Rolle. Writing in graphic, vigorous and colourful language, the author of *The Cloud* teaches a simple method of prayer which takes one directly to God. He writes with an authority that comes from his own personal experience. But he was no maverick. He drew on a well-grounded tradition. He was a teacher who knew his Bible well, and was equally at home with many of the great teachers of Christian spirituality.

Who was he? We don't know his name, and probably never will. Although he wrote seven books, he successfully kept his name a secret even from his contemporaries. But from the dialect in which he wrote we do know that he lived in the East Midlands of England.

He was writing at a time of terrible turbulence and social upheaval. He must have known at first hand the unimaginable disaster of the Black Death, which within the space of two years wiped out no less than one-third of the population of England. It is very likely that he was a Cistercian monk and a priest.

Who was he writing for? In the case of *The Cloud* he was expressly addressing a novice monk or hermit aged 24, and it was also for the same person that he wrote his later book *The Book of Privy Counselling.*[1]

Rediscovery

For several hundred years, *The Cloud* was practically unheard of. It was rediscovered in the nineteenth century, but only came to wider notice through the pioneering work of Evelyn Underhill (1875–1941). Over the last 50 years *The Cloud* has attracted widespread attention among teachers of contemplative prayer, spiritual directors and guides, and among the growing number of people who practise such prayer. There are several factors to account for this. Positively, many thousands of lay people seem to have been naturally drawn to it, when other forms of prayer have gone dead on them. This widespread attraction has been in a large part a response to the even more recent rediscovery of Christian traditions of contemplative prayer by some communities of monks and nuns – traditions that had been almost lost here in the West.

The current climate

It seems also to be true that at a time of increasing restiveness in the Church and some disillusionment with its institutional life many people have found in contemplative prayer a spiritual resource that transcends old denominational divisions. *The Cloud of Unknowing* has been particularly welcomed for its apparent light touch in regard to traditional ritual and dogma. It has an appeal to those who are interested less in organized religion and more in personal spirituality. At first reading it seems to offer a way of connecting, or reconnecting, the individual seeker with God that is not dependent upon bishops or ministers, church tradition or sacraments.

Another factor in its current appeal may be that a deep or wide knowledge of the Bible is not assumed or expected by the author. And where he does use Scripture, he seems to be interested in relatively minor characters, such as the sisters Mary and Martha of Bethany, rather than the major figures – with the exception of Jesus Christ. This aspect gives the book a special attraction to feminists and to those who are looking for alternative readings of biblical texts.

Others again are looking for a way of making links between Christianity and other world faiths. Focusing on the practice rather than on doctrine or philosophy, *The Cloud* is well suited to those looking for a meeting point between Western and Eastern traditions of contemplative prayer.

The scope of this book – and a double danger

In the first six chapters I outline what I believe to be the author's essential teaching. In Chapter 7, in answer to some reservations that have been expressed about *The Cloud* as a resource for the spiritual journey, I discuss whether the prayer he advocates may be called *Christian* prayer in its fullest sense. In my final chapter I describe some of the ways in which contemporary teachers of contemplative prayer are using and adapting the teaching of *The Cloud*, and the emerging possibilities for interfaith dialogue and practice.

Writing this book for publication has been a doubly dangerous, and perhaps even foolhardy, project. The author of *The Cloud* warns his readers 'by the authority of love' not to let his book get into the hands of those who have not committed themselves to be whole-hearted followers of Jesus Christ. Second, he warns his readers to read his book as a whole, and not to be selective and run the peril of distorting or misunderstanding his teaching.

I have taken to heart these two warnings, but have come to the conclusion that at the present time, when sadly there is still not enough understanding of the nature of contemplative prayer in many Christian quarters, the danger of his teaching being misunderstood and misinterpreted is less serious than the danger of it being unknown, unnoticed and unpractised. Although I have been necessarily selective, I have tried to communicate what I believe to be the essential themes of *The Cloud*, omitting what I consider to be less significant topics, or those of historic rather than current interest.

Finally, I would urge all who after reading this book find that they are personally drawn to attempt contemplative prayer to lose no time in acquiring a copy of *The Cloud of Unknowing*, and read it for themselves. And even more strongly I would urge such readers not to delay practising it, preferably by joining a local group of those who are already practising a form of Christian contemplative prayer, in which they will find ongoing mutual support.[2] As with any skill or art, there is absolutely no substitute for regular daily practice.

1

Is contemplative prayer for me?

━━◆◆◆━━

Do I have a desire to pray in this way?

The opening words of *The Cloud of Unknowing* are a prayer to God that will sound more or less familiar to Christians of many traditions:[1]

> God, to whom all hearts are open, and to whom all desires speak, and from whom no secrets are hidden, I beseech you to cleanse my heart's purpose with the inexpressible gift of your grace, so that I may perfectly love you and worthily praise you. Amen.

From the outset, the author of *The Cloud* is at pains to say that without such a desire for an intimate encounter with God, it would be a waste of time even to start on the path of contemplative prayer. Thus the full title of the book is:

> Here Begins a Book of Contemplation called
> The Cloud of Unknowing,
> In which a soul is made one with God

So the first question for his readers is this. Have I that desire for God in me? Now some may know their hearts well enough to discern this desire. For others, perhaps yourself, it may well be the case that you are not yet aware of such a desire. You should not immediately feel put off or discouraged. The very fact that you have picked up this book could be an indication that, although you don't yet have this clear desire, you may have more than a passing wish to do so. Michael Ramsey[2] used to say that sometimes he found it impossible to pray, but as he put time aside for prayer, he would ask God to give him the desire to pray. Even the most experienced contemplatives may feel that they are from time to time once again at the bottom of the ladder.

In his very last chapter,[3] the author again picks up the same theme of 'desires', quoting St Augustine: 'The whole life of a good Christian is nothing but holy desire.' This theme of desire is central to our author's thinking: whether it is desire for God, desire for God's grace, desire for heaven or simply holy desires. How much do I really desire God? That is the big question. It is a theme that runs through the Psalms; for example:

> As a deer longs for flowing streams,
> so my soul longs for you, O God.
> My soul thirsts for God, for the living God.
> When shall I come and behold the face of God?[4]

Our author teaches that contemplative prayer should be attempted only by those who have within them a God-kindled desire, and, in a memorable phrase, a desire to which God has 'fastened a leash of longing.'[5] The word 'leash'[6] is one of our author's many striking images. Anyone who has ever owned or looked after a dog will know the necessity of a leash. However well trained a dog is and however devoted to its master or mistress, there are times and places where it has to be controlled, especially on public roads, for a dog is by nature interested and excited by the sight, sound and scent of other creatures. Without such a restraint, it would run into danger of causing injury or death to itself or others.

But a leash is not a straitjacket, an instrument of total control. Human freedom is not crushed by God's loving and restraining hand. The one holding a leash is just ensuring that the one being restrained is simply going in the right direction. The expression has a biblical echo – one that expresses the same thought of God's guiding and constraining love and compassion: 'When Israel was a child, I loved him, and out of Egypt I called my son . . . I led them with cords of human kindness, with bands of love.'[7] And we recall the words of Jesus to his disciples: 'You did not choose me but I chose you.'[8] It is God who calls us to the practice of contemplative prayer.

A moral commitment

Yet desire alone is not sufficient for a vocation to be clearly discerned. A commitment to persevere in the practice is also essential. 'This desire must always be shaped in your will by the hand of Almighty God and with your own consent.'[9] We shall see later how significant this idea of 'consent' is in some contemporary teachers of contemplative prayer.[10] But for the present we will simply note how our author stresses the need for the co-operation of the human will. Later in his book he defines the will as 'the faculty by which we choose good after it has been identified by [the] reason, and by which we love God, desire God, and finally rest in God with complete joy and consent'.[11] The key idea here is that of human choice. He calls the will the spiritual heart. Here there is more than an echo of St Augustine: 'our hearts are restless until they rest in you'.[12]

In the final two chapters[13] of *The Cloud* the author describes in detail the signs by which a true vocation to contemplative prayer may be discerned.

The signs of a contemplative vocation: inclination of the heart, mind and body

> If it seems to you that this kind of activity does not agree with your inclination in body and soul, you may give it up and safely undertake another way without blame, under the guidance of a reliable spiritual adviser.[14]

Our author emphasizes that contemplative prayer must agree with a person's whole inclination. If there is not yet a strong desire at least there must be an inclination or disposition towards it. And this inclination is one that has to be not only internal and spiritual, but also outward and physical. Here is a thoroughly healthy recognition that nature and grace must be in tandem. A would-be contemplative needs to test that his or her whole personality and make-up – physical, mental and emotional – is one that is comfortable with this kind of prayer. And although contemplative prayer is theoretically possible within and alongside most other human activities, especially walking or standing, most people find that in order to minimize distractions the most suitable posture is sitting still with the eyes closed. The important thing, our author says, is that we should be 'unchangingly restful'.[15]

A pleasurable stirring not enough

Second, he distinguishes between an inclination of the heart and a pleasurable stirring of the mind. The latter he says may come from a natural curiosity – as if one were to say to oneself, 'Now I know what contemplative prayer is about and how to learn it.' This pleasurable stirring is, however, only the intellectual satisfaction that comes from discovering something new. It could be a preparation for a more profound spiritual movement, but it is not the same as a longing of the heart. This comes from a much deeper place within the human personality, that part of us associated with love and passion. Here he is reiterating the point he has already made in his Prologue, that the people he has in mind are not those 'driven by mere curiosity, whether educated or uneducated'.

A variety of contemplative vocations

But our author is far from having an exclusive attitude. From the outset he recognizes that not all contemplatives will be 'full-time specialists'. There are those, whether they are ordinary lay people, ordained ministers or priests, or members of religious communities, who may have this God-given desire for contemplative prayer. He specifically refers to those leading truly good, active lives:

> who though their outward manner of existence belongs to the active life, are nevertheless stirred by the Spirit of God ... to be inclined by grace towards the highest level of contemplative activity – not continually, as is appropriate for true contemplatives, but to share in it now and then.

Thus he leaves it entirely open as to the frequency of such contemplative prayer for Christians whose circumstances make it impossible for them to be 'full-time' contemplatives.

This is a most important principle, to which we shall return later on in this book, when we discuss the two sisters Mary and Martha,[16] and when we look at how contemporary teachers have used and adapted the teaching of *The Cloud*.[17]

Tests for discernment

Returning to the theme of the signs of a contemplative vocation, our author recommends a series of tests for discerning whether there is a true inclination of the heart or only a pleasurable stirring of the mind.[18]

The first test is: 'let them examine whether they have done their best in advance, preparing themselves for it by cleansing their consciences according to the judgement of Holy Church and with the agreement of their advisers'. In other words, we need to check whether we have done our best to prepare ourselves for contemplative practice by examining ourselves, and if necessary seeking absolution from God by going to the sacrament of Reconciliation or Penance, and when appropriate seeking reconciliation with our neighbours. Contemplative prayer requires the blessing of a clean heart, but purity of heart is not possible without a sincere desire to spring-clean our spiritual and moral house. For this test we may find it desirable, even necessary, to seek the help and advice of an experienced spiritual adviser or director.

The second test is this: 'let them examine whether it is always pressing into their minds more habitually than any other kind of spiritual exercise'. If we feel a sense of being drawn, almost pressed, towards contemplative prayer, especially when we are engaged in other forms of prayer, such as petition, intercession or thanksgiving, then this may be another sign of a contemplative vocation. Or do I have a sense that contemplative prayer is 'this secret little thrust of love', the spiritual crown of all my prayer, as it were, towards which all else is leading me? This is a very definite sign of a vocation to contemplative prayer.

Our author now adds an important proviso to be borne in mind by all those who believe themselves to be called to contemplative prayer:

> I do not say that it will always last and remain continually in the minds of all those who are called to this activity. No, it is not like that. For various reasons, the actual feeling is frequently withdrawn from a young spiritual apprentice in contemplation.

And not only young spiritual apprentices, we might add! All spiritual teachers talk about periods when there seems to be no feeling or desire for contemplative prayer, times of dullness or numbness, when the Spirit of God who had once seemed so lively and present appears to be withdrawn. The sixteenth-century founder of the Jesuit order, St Ignatius Loyola, called these times periods of desolation, to be contrasted with times of consolation. A notable recent example is Mother Teresa of Calcutta, whose private journal, published posthumously, revealed that she suffered from the most terrible spiritual desolation, not just for short periods but for very many years.[19]

Our author suggests that there are some very good reasons for this apparently negative experience. The first reason is that it would not be to our advantage to have 'too great a familiarity with it and suppose that it is largely in his own power to have when he pleases and as he pleases'. Such a presumption could well induce in us a feeling of pride, or at least the possibility that pride would develop if the feeling of grace were not withdrawn. There are times when God's grace seems to be absent. Paradoxically, it is often those times of painful desolation that produce greater spiritual growth, not least in our realization of how much we depend upon God's grace.

There is, however, a different cause of this negative experience, which can be very painful in its effect: 'Sometimes it is withdrawn because of their carelessness, and when this happens they soon afterwards feel a most bitter pain that scourges them very hard.' The carelessness may be a moral carelessness, leading to remorse, and a feeling of self-doubt, even self-hatred. Or it could be a spiritual carelessness, a failure to put into effect a discipline of prayer and worship. Whatever the nature of the lapse, immediate steps need to be taken to get back on the road. The loving support of a soul friend or spiritual guide is usually the answer.

Waiting for the gift

A different kind of reason for this withdrawal of desire for contemplation could be similar to the first one – it has nothing at all to do with our weaknesses or faults, but everything to do with God's plan for us: 'Sometimes our Lord will delay it in accordance with a plan, because by the delay he wishes to make it grow and be held in greater esteem.' So we are to be patient. Wait for the Lord and the Lord will surely come. This is the frequently expressed message of the Psalmist, the prophets, Jesus of the Gospels, and the apostles: 'Be still before the LORD, and wait patiently for him';[20] 'But those who wait for the LORD shall renew their strength, they shall mount up with wings like eagles.'[21]

For our author, 'this is one of the most supreme and reliable signs by which a soul may know whether or not he is called to this work'. He explains it like this in a long but perfectly clear and forceful sentence:

> If after such a delay and such lengthy absence of this activity he feels, when it comes suddenly as it does, without the help of any intermediary, that he then has a more burning desire and a greater love-longing to undertake this activity than he had before – so much so that I believe he often has greater joy in finding it than he ever had sorrow in losing it – if this is so, it is surely a true and unquestionable sign that he is called by God to undertake this activity, whatever he may be or may have been.

This is a crucial passage, highly significant for its understanding of the sheer givenness of contemplative prayer. All the great spiritual teachers, especially the Spanish mystics John of the Cross and Teresa of Avila, say the same. While we can certainly develop the skills necessary for contemplative prayer, ultimately such prayer comes as a gift given in response to a desire and a longing that is itself God-given. It is up to us to prepare the ground, and to place ourselves in readiness for God's gift. But in the end it is up to God to give us the gift.

The contemplative Church

If I were to comment here on the main thrust of our author's teaching on vocation I would say this. The calling to contemplative prayer is without a doubt a privileged one. Not all are given it, but undoubtedly there are more vocations than is commonly assumed. It is not such a rare gift as many have thought. There is a strong element of the God-given, but it is in no way an exclusive or elitist club for specialists. And whatever our own vocation may seem to be, there remains this question. Am I ready to acknowledge not just the desirability, but the necessity, of a contemplative dimension in the life of the Church? And if so, what should be my part in encouraging and promoting such a contemplative dimension? One of the greatest theologians of the twentieth century, Karl Rahner, prophesied that 'The Christian of the future will be a mystic or he will not exist at all.'[22] In saying this, Rahner did not mean that all Christians will be having paranormal experiences of lights, visions and voices and so forth. He meant rather that the prayer of silence and stillness, the prayer of listening, the prayer of simply being in the acknowledged presence of God, will become the normative practice and experience of all Christians. If that prophecy comes anywhere near true it will, of course, be a massive revolution.

In whatever way God gives the gift of contemplative prayer, when God gives it, and in whatever form it is given are all within the mysterious hand of God the Holy Spirit. But we do not need to plead for it, only to make ourselves ready for it, and then receive it gladly.

2

One little word

The Cloud: chapters 3, 4, 7, 37, 38

How to approach God

'Lift up your heart towards God'[1] is our author's first advice for anyone wishing to pray. We are immediately reminded of the opening dialogue between the priest and the people at the Eucharist. But at a deeper level we are reminded that any prayer worth the name must engage the heart: that is, not only the emotions, over which we have limited control, but our whole being, our intellect, our will, our body, our whole personality. We are deliberately to turn our attention to God, the One who holds us in his love, and who looks for our response.

To these first six words, he adds, 'with a humble stirring of love'. 'Stirring' is one of his favourite words (we have already met it in a different context[2]). It is variously rendered into modern English as 'impulse', 'movement', 'prompting'.[3] In other words, it is a dynamic force of the human spirit – an opening up, as someone might open up their lungs with a huge inhaling breath, or throw up their arms in joy or triumph. He qualifies this thought of 'stirring' with 'humble', a word that is often misunderstood. It does not mean self-deprecating, or self-abasing. Its root lies in the word 'humus', which as every gardener knows means earth or soil. To be humble is to keep one's feet on the ground. It is to acknowledge one's earthy and bodily nature. We are not angels, we have bodies. As St Francis was fond of saying, our body is all too often an obstinate ass. It will not do what we ask of it, but go its own way. Anyone who is a member of a silent meditation group soon becomes aware that not only do chairs creak but throats cough and tummies rumble.

9

Letting go – letting God

His next advice is: 'Think of God himself, not of anything to be gained from him.' Then he adds:

> See that you refuse to think of anything but him, so that nothing acts in your intellect or will but God himself. And do what you can to forget all of God's creations and all their actions, so that your thoughts and desires are not directed and do not reach out towards any of them, in general or in particular. But leave them alone and pay no heed to them.

Here we come to what is almost certainly the hardest and yet absolutely essential task for anyone setting out on a path of contemplative prayer: the need to let go of all thoughts, ideas, memories, hopes, desires, fantasies, wish-lists – anything that may occupy the mind. The reason for this is that however good some of these may be in themselves, they are all distractions taking us away from what is to be the sole focus of our attention, that is, God. So we are not even to think of God's blessings, God's love, God's holiness, or of the beauty and order of his creation, however marvellous, delightful, glorious or inspiring these may be. We are to focus our whole attention simply on God, just content to be in God's presence. This task of wholehearted attention is not easy, but it is possible.

On the day I am writing this, I heard again the extraordinary story of the deliberate ditching by the pilot of a US Airways Airbus in the Hudson river in which all 155 lives were saved. The pilot had taken off on 16 January 2009 from LaGuardia Airport, New York, when a flock of Canada geese flew into both engines, destroying them immediately. The aircraft was now only going one way – very quickly down to earth. He had no time to return to the airport or to reach any landing place. With no other alternative, and the seconds racing by, he had only one possibility of a safe descent – to bring the aircraft down into the river. Later on he was asked whether in those brief short minutes he had given any thought to the welfare and safety of the passengers. He replied like this: 'No. I had to focus entirely on one task – the task of bringing the aircraft down safely on water. Any thought for the passengers would have prevented me from giving my total attention to my one essential task.'[4]

Contemplative prayer may not require that kind of professional heroism, but it does require our wholehearted attention, such as we would give to any task that requires such intensity. We cannot attempt contemplative prayer on autopilot.

'A naked intent unto God'

These are the striking words that our author uses to describe this formidable task of total attention. Even in Middle English this phrase – another favourite of his – leaps off the page at the reader. It has two related meanings: 'a purpose focussed on God for God's own sake, stripped of self-will and of desire for anything to be gained from him, and also a simple intention stripped of all imagery',[5] that is, any pictures of or ideas or thoughts about God. In other words, we need to give our whole *attention* to God, and also commit our mind, our *intention*, to do so for whatever time it takes.

In comment I would say that contemplative prayer is what an ancient Christian tradition calls 'pure prayer' – as in pure mathematics, where 'pure' means done for its own sake. And we may call to mind the teaching of Jesus in the sixth beatitude: 'Blessed are the pure in heart, for they will see God',[6] where one aspect of purity of heart is simplicity or integrity. And if this ideal seems in practical terms very difficult for us to reach even briefly, because in all human actions mixed motives are the norm, we need to remember that the goal is one that is ultimately promised to all who are blessed with faith, hope and love, especially love.[7] 'For now we see through a glass, dimly, but then' – 'that is, at the End, when God consummates his promises'[8] – 'face to face'.

It was the Trappist monk Thomas Merton, undoubtedly one of the most influential of all teachers of contemplative prayer in the twentieth century, who quoted the mystic Simone Weil[9] as saying that the best definition of prayer is 'absolute attention'.

Extraordinarily difficult yet extraordinarily easy

However diffident we may feel at setting out on this seemingly tough road, the author hastens to reassure his readers by a number of encouragements. First, he says, you are not alone: 'All the saints and angels rejoice in this work, and hasten to help it with all their might.' 'Therefore with angels and archangels and with the whole company of heaven . . .', we say at the heart of the Eucharist, and this is just as true of private prayer. Conversely, he says in his typical way, 'all the devils are driven crazy when you do this and try to frustrate it in all ways that they can'.

A couple of centuries later, the reformer Martin Luther made the comment (quoted by the twentieth-century Christian apologist C. S. Lewis): 'the best way to drive out the devil, if he will not yield to texts of Scripture, is to jeer and flout him, for he cannot bear scorn'.[10] When anyone refuses to be cowed either by the mockery of others or by their own self-doubt, and boldly takes up the call to contemplative prayer, they are embraced by the saints, but their struggle with negativity will continue in new and unpredictable ways.

Second, he says that you have no idea how much your fellow beings around you are being 'marvellously helped by your work, in ways you do not know'. However unseen and insignificant our prayer may seem to be to us, it has a ripple effect, like a stone cast into a pond. The rippled water laps against the pebbles on the shoreline, and in the same way our prayers affect the lives of those around us.

In contrast to the individualism of the modern world, our author sees only interconnectedness. Whether we realize it or not, every human being is part of a network, in which we are constantly interacting with others. He sees contemplative prayer as having a remarkably positive effect on all who practise it, by cleansing us of sin, and even by making us virtuous. Such a claim may strike us at first as an exaggeration, but the personal experience of those who practise contemplative prayer supports it.

When he speaks of the benefits of our prayers for those in purgatory, for some of us he may be opening up a controversial area of debate, but it is better to keep our minds open. It was the experience of the catastrophe of the First World War that changed the minds of Protestants in this respect. Previously strongly opposed to prayers for the dead, many (perhaps most) Protestants came to accept not only their own emotional need to pray for their dead sons and husbands, but also that in praying for them they were entering into the redeeming prayer of the Crucified One who is also victorious over sin and death. Later, we shall return to look in more depth at the question of the *Cloud*-author's understanding of sin and how it is to be overcome.[11]

The substantial point our author is making here is that although he readily admits that the work of contemplative prayer can be 'extraordinarily difficult', yet when we are given the grace of God 'it is the easiest work of all and the soonest completed'. Therefore, he encourages his reader: 'Do not give up, but labour at it until you feel the "stirring"'.

And when we feel that 'stirring', what then? Well, here we come to his central teaching on the efficacy of the one little prayer word.

One little word

In chapter 7 our author puts it like this, and his teaching could not be more simple or direct:

Therefore, whenever you resolve to undertake this work of contemplation, and feel that by grace you are called by God, lift up your heart to God with a humble stirring of love. And think of God who made you and redeemed you, and who has graciously called you to this work, and accept no other thought of God, and do not accept even these thoughts, unless you choose; for a naked intention directed to God is totally sufficient, without any other goal than himself.

If you want to have this intention wrapped and enfolded in one word, so that you can hold on to it better, take only a short word of one syllable; that is better than one of two syllables, for the shorter it is, the better it agrees with the work of the spirit. A word of this kind is GOD or the word LOVE. Choose whichever you wish, or another as you please, whichever you prefer of one syllable, and fasten the word to your heart, so that it never parts from it, whatever happens.

Like other teachers of contemplative prayer, our author is suggesting the most practical way he knows of launching into it. The human mind needs an anchor to hold it still in the rushing waters of the stream of consciousness, in which memories, thoughts, anxieties and plans keep disturbing and distracting it. To achieve that 'naked intention directed towards God', which is the essence of contemplative prayer, we need an actual word to fasten to our heart, preferably a word of one syllable.

We need to take good note here that what is recommended is not a technique by which we can measure our progress. If we think like this, we shall soon become frustrated and disillusioned. There is no ladder by which we climb higher and higher. It is rather a weapon, tool or discipline that enables us to attempt the art of contemplative prayer, at which in this life we for ever remain novices.

How long does it take?

Our author returns to the subject of the one short word in a later chapter, in which he asks the question: 'How long does it take?'[12] He first states that the kind of prayer he advocates is one that takes only 'an instant' – that is, the shortest possible time imaginable. It is interesting that our author's concept of an instant (which he calls an 'atom') was quite precise. Following accepted medieval reckoning, there were 22,560 'atoms' in an hour, so in our current reckoning a little more than 6 every second.

Our author's argument here is, as we have come to expect, completely down to earth:

> If a man or woman is frightened by some sudden occurrence of fire, or of someone's death, or whatever else it may be, then suddenly in the extremity of his spirit he is driven by haste and necessity to shout or beg for help. So how does he do it? Certainly not in many words, or even in words of two syllables . . . and so he bursts out violently in great emotion, and shouts just a short word of one syllable, such as the word FIRE! or the word OUT!

He goes on to argue that 'when a short word of one syllable is not just spoken or thought but secretly intended in the depth of spirit, which is also the height (for in spiritual things it is all the same, height and depth, length and breadth)', then 'it pierces the ears of almighty

God sooner than any long psalm mindlessly mumbled in the mouth. That is why it is written that short prayers pierce heaven.'

What do we make of the practice recommended here, and of his thinking about God's accessibility to human prayer? There will surely be many who will be surprised by, and readily warm to, the robust directness and simplicity of his teaching. Our author understands contemplative prayer not as a pious exercise for the leisured or the super-devout, but as a prayer that arises from a deep longing, a cry in the heart, in some cases perhaps almost a scream.

From darkness to the light of God's presence

Those of us who have meditated for some time may have met people who have recently come out of a very dark place, maybe from depression, or from experiences of drug abuse or alcoholism, or imprisonment, looking for stability and peace in their lives, and have found their way to the practice of silent meditation. From the depths of their being they are literally crying 'Help!' They don't want long prayers. They want to be able to pray, and they are looking to God to help them, to rehabilitate them back into the mainstream of life. So at the human level of practice, our author's approach is sheer common sense. Keep your prayer short – the shorter the better.

If we ask, however, what his theology is, we may get the initial impression that it looks as if he is putting God on a distant throne, accessible only to those who shout loudest. But this is the paradox of prayer. God may seem to be distant, even absent, but this is not the reality, as he has already acknowledged in his opening prayer ('God, to whom all hearts are open, and to whom all desires speak, and from whom no secrets are hidden . . .'[13]). Like many good teachers and preachers, he uses whatever examples from everyday life will best drive home his message. And, as we shall see, his theology consists of a profound recognition that God's existence and every human life are so closely intertwined that they are almost inseparable ('the fact that I exist, Lord, I offer to you, for it is yourself'[14]).

Despite all our deepest fears and imaginings, there is no gap between God and us. As St Augustine put it, 'God is closer to me than I am to myself';[15] or again, 'O Beauty ever ancient, ever new, you were within and I was outside myself'.[16] Our one little word is not so much a shout as a loving word of trust and love, uttered out loud sometimes perhaps, but most often silently in the heart. 'Just as this short word "FIRE!" soon arouses the ears of the listeners, and pierces them more rapidly, so does a short word of one syllable when it is not just spoken or thought but secretly intended in the depth of the spirit.'[17]

The point then is not the vehemence with which this one little word is said, but its origin within that inmost part of the human personality in which we face our deepest hopes and fears. I am reminded of the profoundly moving experience of hearing Archbishop Desmond Tutu preach. It was not so much what he said (although that was unforgettable) but the sense that everything he said came from a deep, praying place in him in which suffering and joy, pain and hope, and indeed every human emotion and reflective thought were located.[18] A memorable saying of his encapsulates that sense: 'A person is a person because he recognizes others as persons.'

'Short prayers pierce heaven'

Our author goes on to develop this point still further in his next chapter. 'And why does it pierce heaven, this short little prayer of one little syllable?'[19] He gives his answer in words that are drawn from the New Testament:[20] 'Surely because it is prayed with a full heart, in the height and the depth, the length and the breadth of the spirit of the person who prays.' According to an interpretation of this text that goes back to St Bernard of Clairvaux, two centuries before *The Cloud* was written, 'length' refers to the eternity of God, 'breadth' to God's love, 'height' to God's power, and 'depth' to God's wisdom. But how can these terms refer to a human being? Because, says our author, 'a soul which is so nearly conformed by grace to the image and likeness of God, its maker, is soon heard by God'; so much so, in fact, that even 'a very sinful soul – an enemy to God – if it could through grace manage to shout such a little syllable in the height and depth, the length and breadth of its spirit, would always be heard and helped by God.'

This is an astonishingly positive understanding of the efficacy of the longing for union with God articulated through the medium of this short prayer word. Such a longing, wholeheartedly and sincerely articulated in that one word, can swiftly overcome years of alienation from God. Like St Paul, our author believes that ultimately nothing can separate those who are faithful to Christ from the love of God.[21] So this one short prayer word, whether said quietly in deep trust or shouted in anxious desperation, breaks down any apparent barrier between us and God. With all the qualifications described in our first chapter concerning the question of who is called to contemplative prayer, the amazing truth is that such prayer is by no means reserved for the members of a spiritual elite, but in God's generosity is available to all who call upon him.

One important practical question remains from this discussion. How often is this one little word to be prayed? Whenever an aspiration to be united to God is felt? As frequently as is practically possible? The question is left open. This may be because both he and his disciple had a common understanding about the conditions and the opportunities available to them in the context of a hermitage or of an enclosed religious community. This is not the case for ordinary Christians today, living in a totally different social context. We will come back to this in our final chapter when we look at how the teaching of *The Cloud* has been adapted for our own time.

3

Two clouds

The Cloud: chapters 3–9, 12, 14, 26, 28, 31, 32, 43, 59

By love not by thought

The cover of the latest Penguin edition of *The Cloud of Unknowing*[1] shows a medieval illumination of the Trinity.[2] Within a brightly coloured orange oval frame God the Father, richly robed in red gown and purple full-length cloak, is holding up the cross on which the crucified Son is hanging. The Holy Spirit in the form of a dove with outstretched wings is perched on top of the cross, just below the long beard of God the Father. Around the rim of the oval frame are angels in the form of numerous cherubic heads clustering together like billowing clouds. Using imagery taken from earthly life, the artist has tried to communicate the heavenly majesty, the spiritual power and the loving humility of God – the God who took human flesh in Jesus Christ and died to save suffering and sinful human beings. We can truly say that the triune God whom Christians worship is like that.

But here is the paradox. No one has seen God at any time, and God himself cannot be compared to anything on earth. No image of God can possibly do more than point to a reality that is beyond all human description. God has revealed himself in Jesus Christ, but God himself is still beyond every image, concept or formulation.

'But now you ask me, "How am I to think of God himself, and what is he?" And to this I can only answer, "I do not know".'[3] So too the *Cloud*-author invites his disciple to have a healthy agnosticism about what God is like, and to admit that God is quite beyond our human comprehension. However clever or ingenious we are, we can never enter into union with God by thinking of him or about him.

There is, in fact, he teaches, only one way of becoming united to God, and that is by the way of love: the love that God has for us, and the reciprocal love which we can, in the grace of God, give to God. So he writes: 'Of God himself no one can think . . . for he [God] can well be loved, but he cannot be thought. By love he can be grasped and held, but by thought neither grasped nor held.'[4]

The way forward, then, is 'with a sharp dart of longing love'. Again he drives his message home:

> it is possible to have full knowledge of all other created things and their works, and indeed of the works of God himself, and to think clearly about them . . . [but] you must step above it [such knowledge] stoutly but deftly, with a devout and delightful stirring of love, and struggle to pierce that darkness above you; and do not give up, whatever happens.[5]

It is love and love alone that can bring about union with God. Love alone provides the passport to heaven, but the way ahead is a way of darkness, a way of unknowing, a way of dispossession.

The cloud of unknowing

Thus we come to the *Cloud*-author's central image: the first cloud he describes, the cloud of unknowing. The author at once acknowledges a difficulty in plainly describing the cloud of unknowing. He calls it 'a darkness, and as it were a cloud of unknowing, you do not know what'. The only certainty is that when you reach it, you feel in your 'will' a naked, a single-minded, purpose ('intent') towards God.

At the end of chapter 4 he spells out more clearly what he means by the cloud of unknowing:

> Do not suppose, because I call it a darkness or a cloud, that it is a cloud condensed out of the vapours that float in the air, or a darkness like that in your house at night when your candle is out. By intellectual ingenuity you can imagine such a darkness or cloud brought before your eyes on the brightest day in summer, just as conversely you can imagine a clear shining light . . . That is not what I mean. For when I say darkness I mean an absence

of knowing, in the sense that everything you do not know, or have forgotten, is dark to you, because you cannot see it with your mind's eye. And for this reason it is not called a cloud in the air but a cloud of unknowing that is between you and your God.

Thus we need to understand that we enter into the cloud of unknowing not by an act of the imagination or by mental application, but by a desire for God, which brings about a darkness of the mind, a not-knowing, because you cannot 'see' anything with your 'mind's eye'.[6] When you come into this darkened state of mind you are entering a sphere that is beyond all human comprehension or description.

Although the author may perhaps give the impression that he speaks of this cloud in a tentative manner, he is in fact on solid biblical ground. His feet are firmly planted in the story of Moses, especially as interpreted by early Christian commentators. In his seminal *Life of Moses*, for example, St Gregory of Nyssa[7] viewed Moses' calling and career as a parable of the journey of the Christian soul in its search for God.

So, for Gregory, the cloud that led the Israelites through the wilderness was no ordinary cloud. He says: 'It was something beyond human comprehension . . . offering a shelter against the noonday sun, and at night it became a fire leading them with its own light from sunset to sunrise.' Then as they approached Mount Sinai, 'the clear light of the atmosphere was darkened so that the mountain became invisible, wrapped in a dark cloud'.[8] Gregory comments on Moses' experience on the mountain:[9]

> Moses . . . boldly approached the very darkness itself and entered the invisible things . . . After he entered the inner sanctuary of the divine mystical doctrine, there, while not being seen, he was in the company of the Invisible. He teaches, I think, by the things he did that one who is going to associate intimately with God must go beyond all that is visible and, lifting up his own mind, as to a mountain-top, to the invisible and incomprehensible, believe that the divine is there where the understanding does not reach.

For readers today who are unfamiliar with such a way of reading Scripture, an interpretation like this may seem strange. It would not, however, have seemed so to St Paul[10] and the rabbinic tradition he followed. Jewish rabbis, and subsequent Christian teachers, took for granted the possibility of an allegorical method of interpretation of Scripture. Teachers like Gregory of Nyssa argued that the allegorical or mystical reading was to be preferred when the literal reading of Scripture made little sense, or when it offered very little spiritual food. In other words, they were investing their reading with a meaning that corresponded with their own lived experience, and in so doing they were reading Holy Scripture in a way that elicited profound spiritual truths.

The author of *The Cloud* was familiar with this method of reading Scripture. Like other monks of his day, as well as the daily reading of the Psalms and Scripture in the divine offices, he would have regularly practised *lectio divina*. In *lectio divina* (which he refers to in chapter 35), a monk was expected to read a passage of Scripture very slowly until a particular phrase, word or sentence drew his attention, then to stay with this word, chewing on it like a cow chewing the cud, until it became the word of God for him on that day. In so doing the monk was being taught to read Scripture in a way that fed him with sustenance for his daily journey. Nowadays this method of Bible study is both practised within religious communities and widely taught and used in churches and retreat centres.

The image of a soul's ascent up a spiritual mountain towards God is a commonplace idea among spiritual teachers. It was one that the *Cloud*-author would certainly have been familiar with. The image that interests him, however, is not that of an ascent but one of a cloud of darkness and unknowing. Later on he spells out at length some of the difficulties of using the word 'up' when speaking of the spiritual journey.[11] For this cloud of unknowing, he says, is in fact not distant, but very close, much closer than we might think. In fact, the distance between us and the cloud of unknowing, and therefore between us and God, is not great at all. What creates the distance between us and God is our inability, or perhaps our unwillingness, to let go of the thoughts and ideas that inhabit our minds.

The cloud of forgetting

Here lies the significance of the second cloud that our author describes – the cloud of forgetting, into which we are to tread down or with which we are to cover all our thoughts, ideas and images. He writes:

> Perhaps it will seem to you that you are far distant from God because the cloud of unknowing is between you and him, but in fact, rightly understood, you are much further from him when you have no cloud of forgetting between you and everything that was ever created.[12]

From where does he get this image of the second cloud? The term 'cloud of forgetting' was probably coined by the twelfth-century Scottish theologian and spiritual teacher Richard of St Victor. In his book *Benjamin Major* the cloud of forgetting is presented as the symbol of a profound but passive self-forgetfulness in the final steps of the soul's ascent to contemplating God.[13] Our author was familiar with this, for probably the first book he wrote was his English version of Richard of St Victor's companion book *Benjamin Minor*.

The *Cloud*-author's use of the term 'cloud of forgetting' is a more radical one than Richard's. It is concerned not with the *final* steps of the soul's ascent to God, but with a definite act of the will that must be activated *right at the start* of the contemplative exercise. The clue to what he means can be found in the opening paragraph of his paraphrase of *The Mystical Theology of St Denis*, where he writes:

> whenever by the stirring of divine grace you set yourself to undertake the active exercise of your blind contemplation, see that with strong, prudent and eager contrition you forsake your bodily senses (namely hearing, sight, smell, taste and touch), and also your spiritual senses, otherwise known as your intellectual activities; and all things that can be known inwardly by your spiritual senses; and all things that do not now exist, or that may exist in the future though they do not now exist.[14]

By talking of dropping all our thoughts and 'bodily and spiritual senses' beneath a cloud of forgetting our author is referring to the immensely difficult but necessary task facing any would-be contemplative.

When trying to contemplate God's being, how on earth does one deal with the many mental distractions that occur? Though he uses a variety of active verbs, his meaning is always the same. You must put a thick cloud of forgetting between you and everything that has ever been made. You must tread them down, trample them under, hide them, cover them with a thick cloud of forgetting. Treat them during the time of your contemplative 'work' as if they did not exist: a deliberate act of abandoning, shelving, putting out of reach all thoughts, calculations, ideas, imaginings, hopes, fears, dreams and the rest of one's normal mental activity. You are to become totally self-forgetful.

The need for perseverance

Our author readily acknowledges the psychological difficulty of this process: 'Anyone who habitually practises this work will unquestionably find it laborious, yes, very laborious indeed, unless he receives special grace, or else has been practising for a long time.' It is not only the initial act of will that is required, but the perseverance involved throughout the exercise.[15]

Here he offers comfort and assurance. First, it is God who has called you to this task, and he does not fail to help those whom he has called to any particular task. Second, from time to time God gives to contemplatives a glimpse of himself, breaking through the cloud of unknowing, as it were, and even inspiring indescribable and passionate feelings of devotion. It is as if God takes over, and you become aware simply of God's loving care and grace – of the great gift of prayer that God is giving you.

Do you not see how he is standing and waiting for you? For shame! Work hard only a little while, and the greatness and the difficulty of this labour will soon be eased. For though it may be hard and rigorous at first, when you have no devotion, later, when you have devotion, what was very hard before will be made very restful and easy for you, and you will feel either little effort or none at all. For then God will sometimes do all the work himself ... then perhaps he will at times send out a beam of spiritual light, piercing this cloud of unknowing between you and him . . . Then you will sense your feelings aflame with the fire of his love, far more than I can, may, or will tell you at this time.[16]

It is not often that our author writes of heightened feelings of the spirit in this way. No doubt he is wary of giving such intense feelings much weight, because of their transience, their unreliability and the dangers of self-dramatization and self-deceit. Against these difficulties that can prove to be so discouraging he wisely recognizes that such feelings can indeed come from God, and bring refreshment and consolation. There can be little doubt that he speaks from his own personal experience.

Serious distractions

The author also has particular advice for those who feel deeply troubled by the memories of past deeds, or 'any new thoughts or sinful stirrings [which] keep on pressing into your consciousness between you and your God'. His general advice is as always to 'trample upon them vigorously with a fervent stirring of love and tread them down beneath your feet, and to try to cover them with a thick cloud of forgetting, as if they had never been done by you or anyone else on earth'. And if they often rise up, 'push them down as often as they rise'.

He acknowledges that to take such a vigorous course may not always work. In fact, as we shall see, contemporary teachers counsel a gentler approach to distractions, whether trivial or serious.[17]

In such a case of really painful and continuous distractions, he advises two possible stratagems to counter them. The first is 'to pretend not to know that they are pressing so hard upon you, between you and your God, and try to look over their shoulders, as it were, searching for something else – and that something is God, enclosed in a cloud of unknowing'.[18] He has found this stratagem to be effective, he says, because it is simply reinforcing your longing desire for God. He says that such a desire is based on charity, so 'it always merits relief'. Perhaps we might also add that it is a movement of faith that counters our natural fear of failure.

The second technique he recommends is a surprisingly desperate one!

> When you feel that you are quite unable to push them down, cower down before them like a wretched coward overcome in battle, and think it is foolish for you to strive against them any longer, and therefore, in the hands of your enemies, you surrender yourself to God.

What he is recommending is in fact an exercise in humility. Admit that you are beaten, admit that you have no strength to overcome these distractions, and simply turn to God in hopeless despair. It is then, he assures us, that God will come to your rescue, 'take you up and tenderly dry the eyes of your spirit, as the father does with the child that is about to perish in the mouths of wild swine or frenzied biting bears'.

Reflective meditation

We come now to our final question. How can a requirement to cease from all mental activity be compatible with the journey of faith? To put the point more sharply, surely time spent in meditating on God's love, God's beauty and many wonderful examples of his kindness cannot but be time well spent. Yes, that it is true. But the point he is making is that by going down the road of reflective meditation we will never arrive at the goal of our desire. If we wish to find God, we must choose the more difficult path of renouncing all thoughts. For, and this is absolutely central and is worth repeating, as our author does, God cannot be grasped by thought, only by love.

Earlier in the book our author explains the way our minds trick us into taking the wrong path.[19] The unwanted thought is personified as being like an acquaintance or friend who is out to divert us and distract us when we are engaged on an important and urgent mission. So he writes:

> And if any thought rises up and keeps wanting to force itself above you, between you and that darkness, and asks you, 'What are you seeking, and what would you have?' [just] say that it is God you would have: 'I want him, I seek him, and nothing but him.' And if it asks you what that God is, say that it is God who

made and redeemed you, and who has graciously called you to his love; and say that you have no understanding of him. And therefore say, 'Get back down', and tread the thought down firmly with a stirring of love, even though it seems to you most holy, and as though it would help you to seek God.

This is a fine example of how the *Cloud*-author gives his readers an imaginary conversation, which describes accurately what is going on in our heads. We face a conflict between two voices: in this case a conflict between what we *think* would benefit us, and what *actually* would help us. If we let ourselves listen to the siren voice, 'it desires nothing better, for it will chatter more and more', 'bringing you first to a remembrance of Christ's Passion' [and what could be more salutary than that?], then it will let you see the 'wonderful kindness of God' [better still], and soon after this you will be put in mind of 'your old sinful way of life' [wonderful!], and finally you will be reminded of 'some places where you used to live in the past' [Oh, no!]. So, he adds, 'in the end, before you know it, you will be scattered, you do not know where'. In other words, you will be all over the place, completely off course. And the reason for this is very simple: 'you first listened willingly to the thought, answered it, accepted it, and let it work freely'.

He goes on to explain that there was nothing wrong in itself with your train of thought ('what it said was good and holy'). To be a contemplative, you actually do need to develop your spiritual life by reflecting on the truths of the Christian faith. In fact, if you don't, you will certainly go wrong. We really do need lots of practice in such reflective meditation. But this is the challenge. If we wish to begin on the path into contemplative prayer, we must leave all such meditations, all thoughts and imaginings behind. We have to 'push them and hold them down, far beneath the cloud of forgetting, if ever we are to pierce the cloud of unknowing between ourselves and God'.

Strike the cloud

The only thought that we do not leave behind is the thought of God himself, who has called us to this work. And that is where the 'one little word' comes in, as we have already seen. We are to wrap up and enfold our 'naked intent' (single-minded intention) directed towards God in this one word, and 'fasten this word to our heart, so that it never parts from it, whatever happens'. The word he suggests, you will remember from the preceding chapter, is a little but powerful word of one syllable, such as 'GOD' or 'LOVE':

> This word is to be your shield and spear, whether you ride in peace or war. With this word you are to beat on [strike] the cloud and the darkness above you. With this word you are to hammer down every kind of thought beneath the cloud of forgetting, so if any thought forces itself on you, answer it with no more than this one word.

4

Two sisters

———•◆•———

The Cloud: chapters 16–23

Now as they went on their way, [Jesus] entered a certain village, where a woman named Martha welcomed him into her home. She had a sister named Mary, who sat at the Lord's feet and listened to what he was saying. But Martha was distracted by her many tasks; so she came to him and asked: 'Lord, do you not care that my sister has left me to do all the work by myself? Tell her then to help me.' But the Lord answered her, 'Martha, Martha, you are worried and distracted by many things; there is need of only one thing. Mary has chosen the better part, which will not be taken away from her'.[1]

The *Cloud*-author obviously loved this story of the two sisters, busy Martha and quiet Mary, and his teaching about them is a fascinating illustration of his basic thesis. He retells Luke's story in his own words, drawing out what he sees as its essential lesson. Time spent in silence and stillness in the Lord's presence is better than time spent in active service, even though such service is 'very good and very holy'.[2]

Actives and contemplatives

His teaching here is by no means new. St Augustine used the same story to teach the difference between the contemplative life and the active life, and the superiority of the former. In his book *The City of God* he developed this argument still further. He distinguished three kinds of Christian life: the contemplative, the busy or active, and the life that combines the two. In later centuries, other teachers also used the example of the sisters to distinguish two different ways of knowing God. Their basic argument is that the contemplative way is the better one because only in the prayer of contemplation can a person, so far as is possible in this life, be *made one with God*. If the goal of every human life is to be at one with God in eternal bliss, what better preparation could there be on this earth than a life given to the contemplation of the mystery of God?

However, to this traditional idea of the superiority of the contemplative way over the active life, most modern Western Christians are likely to have objections for a whole variety of reasons. We shall discuss this further later in this chapter.

Nevertheless, if we were to think that the author's teaching here was uncontroversial in his own time, we would be mistaken. The teachers may have taught one thing, but the rank and file of the ordinary Christian population thought quite differently. Indeed, this was also true of the religious communities that put good works of charity at the forefront of their programme and lifestyle. They were often deeply suspicious of those who took the path of contemplation. So he says that 'just as Martha complained about her sister Mary, so to this day all actives criticize contemplatives'. In fact he goes further. Whenever anyone feels called to the contemplative life and to abandon all outward occupations, their family and even their closest friends 'will turn on them . . . and tell them that what they are doing is nothing. And immediately they will gather up many untrue stories about the fall of men and women who have devoted themselves to this way of life in the past; and never a good story of those who stand fast'.[3]

Our author expresses his opinion here with particular force, and he believes that he has good reasons for doing so. He feels that those who take up a contemplative vocation have always been at the receiving end of ignorant prejudice and hostility. While he is ready enough to admit that some contemplatives have gone astray, this is no reason for treating the calling to contemplative prayer as nonsense. The calling itself is God's calling, and in his view no calling can be higher than a life devoted to the pure prayer of the contemplation of God. When contemplatives go adrift it is because they have failed to follow the spiritual advice given to them – hence (though he himself does not say this) the importance of the advice he is giving to his readers.

'The better part'

The author wishes us to be absolutely clear about the essential truth that Jesus is pointing to when he told Martha that Mary had chosen 'the better part'. So what was 'the better part'? What precisely was the nature of Mary's occupation when she sat at Jesus' feet, listening to what he was saying to her? It is here that a modern reader will be most challenged. It would be easy to misunderstand. When Mary sat in the presence of Christ, she was not engaged in holy thoughts, nor was she dreaming of heaven, she was *listening*. Who was she listening to? To Jesus, yes, but are we to understand that this is simply a case of a disciple imbibing the spiritual wisdom being offered to her by her teacher?

What did St Luke mean his readers to understand? Jesus' observation that 'Mary has chosen the better part, which will not be taken away from her' is clearly intended as a momentous saying. Jesus is not simply stating that listening to him is a more worthwhile occupation than preparing a good meal for him. That would be churlish. He is rather pointing to the fact that the love of God sometimes requires us to be still and quiet rather than to be overly concerned with distracting practicalities – distractions that may take the mind from the deeper realities of our relationships. Martha was distracted by her many tasks, we are told, and loses her 'cool' with her sister, expecting Jesus to side with her. Tensions have risen, and we have the makings of a family row.

Our author, however, sees much more in this 'everyday story of Bethany folk' than a clash of temperaments. For him it is a paradigm of the contemplative vocation: a superb example of his fundamental thesis that if we are prepared to renounce all our thoughts and ideas and simply attend to the supreme wisdom of God, loving union may be found with God in this life.

Jesus Man and God

So he writes: 'she [Mary] attended only to the supreme wisdom of his Godhead cloaked within the dark words of his Manhood'.[4] He wants us to understand that Mary in her silent prayer in Jesus' presence was engaging with the whole mystery of the One who is both true God and true Man. The essential point here is that in the work of contemplative prayer the mind and heart need to be removed from mental reflection on the human personality of Christ and to turn to the more profound, loving contemplation of his divinity. He writes of Mary: 'I believe she was so deeply moved by love of his Godhead that she paid only the smallest regard to the beauty of his precious and blessed body, that beloved body in which he dwelt',[5] and again she 'paid no attention . . . to the excellence of his blessed body, nor to the sweet voice and words belonging to his Manhood'.[6]

Here we may note how ready our author is to echo the devotional words of his medieval contemporaries who practised and taught a loving and tender approach to the humanity of the suffering and compassionate Jesus, whose images in the form of statues and paintings were to be found so widely in their churches. He does not deny their value, but at the same time he is absolutely clear that once anyone begins on the contemplative path they need to leave behind all images and thoughts in order to enter into the pure prayer of the heart.

What the *Cloud*-author is doing here is speaking out of his own personal experience of contemplative prayer. It is evident that he sees Mary as the prototype of everyone and anyone who is called to the contemplative life.

Martha's worries and distractions

What, then, of Martha? Our author notices that in the Gospel story, when Martha entered the room to complain to the Lord about her sister, Mary kept to her task, refusing to be distracted. 'She continued to pray.' In this respect Mary may be contrasted with her sister who, we are told, was 'worried and distracted by her many tasks'.

Of course, it is natural for us to feel sympathetic with Martha's feelings. It was her duty and her pleasure as hostess to do the best she could for her honoured guest. She felt left in the lurch by her sister's lack of support. In her stress, she became overwhelmed by a sense of unfairness.

Our author is, however, not so interested in the relationship of the sisters as we might be, nor does he take sides in what could turn out to be an unprofitable and stale argument. Nevertheless, he is concerned to defend Martha against unfair criticism. So he affirms Martha as 'that special saint'.[7] Her active life of service for the Lord is not in question. And he judges Martha's complaint about Mary as perfectly natural, given her ignorance of Mary's contemplative 'work' when she sat at Jesus' feet. Thus everyone called to the active life should readily be pardoned when they complain about contemplatives, just as our author would hope and pray to be pardoned for his own innumerable faults 'that I myself have committed in the past out of a lack of knowledge'. In his opinion Martha has not yet learned what Mary has already discovered: that a life of service, however excellent it is, is no substitute for a life of loving contemplation of God. So when Jesus hears Martha's complaint he not only defends Mary when she is under attack, he also uses the opportunity gently to offer appropriate spiritual counsel to Martha. Indeed, through the medium of Scripture he offers guidance to all who think that a life of active service could be of equal value to, or even higher value than, the contemplative life.

Mary's prayer

Furthermore, when Mary is commended by the Lord, our author must have had in mind that she was doing exactly what his own novice monk is being trained to do. In a beautiful phrase our author writes: 'she is hanging her love and her longing desire on this cloud of unknowing'. Even though she may *appear* to be sitting quite still in her 'rest and ease', as he puts it later,[8] Mary is far from idle. In fact, he implies that she is working just as hard as her sister – perhaps even harder – but her work is different. It is a work requiring constant attention, discarding all unwanted thoughts, all superficial emotions. She is teaching 'herself to love something in this life she could not see clearly in her reason by the light of understanding, nor yet feel truly in her emotions in the sweetness of love'.[9] The Mary of this story may not yet fully know God, for God remains beyond the grasp of all human knowledge, but her contemplative prayer is nevertheless 'the better part'. This is because she is looking in the right direction, and above all she is looking towards God with little silent, loving words that arise from her heart. So he writes:

> to that wisdom of Christ's Godhead . . . she attended with all the love of her heart. From that, she would not be diverted by anything she saw or heard spoken or done around her but sat with her body quite still, with many sweet secret and eager thrusts of love into that high cloud of unknowing between her and her God.[10]

Some broader implications

There is something more to be said. Our author is convinced that there are lessons here for those engaged in the active life as well as the contemplative life. Just as the Lord rebuked Martha when she complained about her sister, he strongly urges those called to the active life to get on with their own 'business (busyness)', and not to complain about those who are called to a life of contemplation.[11]

And his advice to those called to such a life of contemplative prayer is to follow Mary's exemplary behaviour when her sister complained. He says, 'if we pay no more attention to their words or their thoughts than she did, and no more abandon our secret spiritual work, then our Lord will answer them in spirit and . . . they will be ashamed of their words and thoughts'. His message is that contemplatives should look to the Lord for support. They do not need to defend themselves. In the end they will be vindicated.

Our author further comments that it is a mistake to think that no one should commit themselves to contemplative life unless they have been assured of the supply of basic necessities such as food and clothes.[12] Either God will find a way of supplying them with their needs or else, failing that, he will give them the strength of body and spiritual fortitude to put up with their lack. In this respect our author was nearer to the teaching (and practice) of our Lord in the Sermon on the Mount[13] than to the contemporary ecclesiastical rules with regard to hermits, which restricted the contemplative vocation to those who were assured of material support. Our author, however, is not concerned any more than Jesus is with laying down prudential rules, as a bishop, abbot or abbess might feel obliged to do.[14] He is rather setting goals, as any good teacher does for his students – goals that call in this context for qualities of courage and wholeheartedness.

Then and now

How, then, are we in our own time and circumstances to apply our author's interpretation of the Martha and Mary story? In answering that question, we may well find ourselves questioning some of our author's basic assumptions.

As has already been observed, he followed St Augustine and many of the medieval teachers in his conviction that the contemplative life is the highest calling anyone may have. This conviction is stated clearly in his very first chapter, and is reiterated frequently. He also assumed that in order to fulfil the contemplative vocation it is first necessary to have embraced the active life, and then in due course to leave the lay, active life and enter into a religious order or become a recognized hermit or anchoress, such as Julian of Norwich.

Today many would question the idea of a natural progression from the active life to the contemplative life. It is possible that an active life of service makes sense for physically healthy people in their early or middle adulthood, while a contemplative life may be more suitable for people who are older or who are perhaps physically disabled. However, such a broad generalization can easily be misunderstood. A contemplative life is never to be seen as a substitute for an active life, but rather as a necessary complement to it throughout the whole of life. We know that our author's disciple was a young man of 24 years, and in every generation young men and women continue to be called to a contemplative life.

Moreover, the calling to a life of contemplative prayer or, more commonly today, a life that is a mixture of outward service and contemplative prayer, is not an exclusive calling for the especially devout. It is a challenge to every follower of Christ to take seriously the possibility of giving contemplative prayer a significant place in their lives – to respect and love Mary as much as Martha. Martha and Mary are not foes, strangers or even in competition with each other (any more than the activist Peter and the contemplative John the

Evangelist are). All four characters are essential. They represent the active and the contemplative parts both of ourselves personally and of our churches, in which neither sister (nor apostle) should be dominant. They can, indeed, work in perfect partnership. But in our present, activist age, when silence and stillness are especially difficult to attain, the Mary and John in all of us and in our churches need extra special care and attention if they are to flourish. In that sense, if in no other, Jesus' words commending Mary for having chosen 'the better part' could well be heard as a clarion call that requires of us all, whoever we are, an immediate and personal response.

5

Two virtues

The Cloud: chapters 2, 12–15, 24, 25

In the last chapter, readers may have noticed how much importance the *Cloud*-author gives to the virtues of both humility and charity in the character of Mary of Bethany. This is no accident. He regards these two virtues as fundamental to human living, and also to the practice of contemplative prayer. So he writes, 'anyone who could acquire these two would clearly need no others, for he would have them all'.[1] Following St Augustine, he defines virtue as 'nothing but an ordered and controlled love, simply directed towards God for himself'.[2] He also argues that if anyone is moved to acquire any virtue by a goal or reason other than God himself, then that virtue remains imperfect. For virtue to be pure or perfect there can be only one motive, which is that it is done for the love of God alone. So to seek virtue because of fear, or for the sake of one's reputation, or of one's career, is to seek it for superficial or inadequate reasons. Such virtue is, in his words, 'imperfect'. However, as we shall see, even some kinds of 'imperfect' virtue can be good up to a point.

First let us look at what he says about humility and then we will examine his writing on charity.

Humility

Right from the beginning of *The Cloud*, its author makes it clear that no progress is possible in the art of contemplative prayer without humility. Thus in the opening sentence of his second chapter, pulling no punches, he addresses his disciple:

Look up now, weak wretch and see what you are. What are you,
and what have you deserved, to be called like this by our Lord?
What kind of heart is it, weary, wretched and slothfully sleeping
that is not aroused by the pull of this love and the voice of this
calling?

I would not be surprised if you are a little put off here by our author's
language and tone. Who likes being addressed as 'weak wretch'? He
sounds rather like the headmaster of an earlier generation addressing his most recalcitrant pupil! But we need to recognize that to his
contemporaries his language would not have seemed unacceptable or
abusive. It is part of a wisdom tradition that goes back to the Scriptures
that the speaker talks 'straight' to his hearers. The context is also worth
some close attention.

In his first chapter, our author has held up before his disciple the
nature of the high calling to which he has been invited by God, and has
emphasized what a great privilege it is to be called to be a contemplative. In this second chapter, he goes on to warn him most strictly 'not
to think of yourself any holier or better because this calling is so
noble . . . but think yourself all the more wretched and accursed unless
you do the best you can to live in accordance with your vocation'.
And to this moral exhortation to embrace humility he adds, in words
that echo various texts in the New Testament, 'you should be all the
humbler and more loving towards your spiritual bridegroom, because
he, almighty God, King of Kings and Lord of lords, was willing to
humble himself so deeply towards you . . . to choose you to be one
of his intimates'. So humility in conduct is best founded on a heartfelt acknowledgement of Christ's own humility, who 'emptied himself,
taking the form of a slave . . . And . . . humbled himself and became
obedient to the point of death – even death on a cross'.[3]

Humility as self-knowledge

We turn now to chapters 13 to 15, in which our author gives his most
extensive treatment of the virtue of humility. He defines humility 'as
being nothing else but one's knowledge and feeling of oneself as one
is; for certainly anyone who could truly see and feel himself as he is
would be truly humble'.

There are two points here to note. Our author always prefers the Anglo-Saxon word to the Latin, and the term he actually uses for humility is 'meekness'. 'Meek' is one of those words whose meaning has changed over the years. Today, if used at all, it would usually suggest someone who is mild, gentle and submissive to a fault, someone who would not say 'boo to a goose'. But in its original usage meekness is a quality that is perfectly compatible with toughness, standing up for oneself and fighting for justice. Sir Thomas Malory, the fifteenth-century author of *Le Morte d'Arthur*, ascribes to Sir Lancelot all the sterling qualities a knight should have, including being at the same time 'sternest knight to thy mortal foe' and also 'meekest of men'. This usage carried on into Shakespeare, where Duncan, the avenger of Macbeth, is described as 'meek'. So too, in the King James Version of the Bible Jesus describes himself as 'meek and lowly in heart' (Matthew 11.29), and even more famously pronounces as blessed 'the meek: for they shall inherit the earth' (Matthew 5.5).

In this context meekness is the quality of being unassuming, not presumptuous, not expecting privileges or favours because of one's birth, rank or achievements, but rather accepting oneself as one really stands, in the sight of God, without illusion or fantasy. It is the quality that leads one 'to inheriting the earth', that is, entry into the Promised Land where the world will be transformed by God into God's kingdom. It is perfectly illustrated in Jesus' parable by the attitude of the publican who saw himself as totally undeserving of God's favour, rather than the 'good' but self-satisfied Pharisee.[4]

It is hardly a surprise, therefore, that our author defines the essential quality of meekness in *The Cloud* as self-knowledge: the ability to appreciate in equal measure what is within one's capability under God's grace, and the weaknesses and habitual sins that hinder one from reaching one's capability. A central principle in the Christian tradition (and incidentally one that can be traced back to the oldest traditions among the ancient Greeks) is that no one can make progress in this life, let alone know God, if he or she has little or no such self-knowledge. St Augustine lamented that it took him so long to find God, because he was, as he put it, outside himself, not yet grounded and centred.[5] He declared: 'Man must first be restored to himself that, making himself as it were a stepping stone, he may rise thence and be borne up to God.'[6]

The second point to note is that *knowing* oneself is not in itself quite enough. Our author repeatedly links such knowledge of oneself with 'feeling oneself' (or, as other modern versions have it, 'being aware' of oneself). In this way, he is broadening out what could be seen as a merely intellectual understanding of oneself to a more basic self-awareness. To use the language of contemporary neurological science, it is the self-knowledge that comes from both sides of the brain, the intuitive as much as the analytical. So he is suggesting that humility is a gift and grace that belongs to the whole personality – not only to the rational thinking side, but equally to the instinctive emotional and relational side.

Perfect and imperfect humility

There are two reasons, our author explains, why we need to be humble. The first arises from our 'impurity, wretchedness and weakness into which we are fallen by sin, and which we must always feel to some degree while we live on earth, however holy we may be'. The second reason is 'the superabundant love and excellence of God in himself, at the sight of which all nature trembles, all scholars are fools, and all saints and angels are blind'.[7] Two beautiful sentences, concisely and memorably put.

In more prosaic words, the first reason is the moral gap between the holy and righteous God and sinful and unrighteous humanity. The second reason is the essential and unavoidable gap between the finite creature and the infinite and eternal Creator; between that which might not have existed, and that which is pure Being, eternal and uncreated. The second reason he calls 'perfect' because 'it will last eternally'. The first reason he calls 'imperfect' because 'it will cease at the end of this life'. In other words, perfect humility will never cease for it will continue throughout the state of eternal bliss. Imperfect humility belongs only to our present earthly condition. So long as we are here on earth and as long as we are aware of our moral fragility, perfect humility is beyond and outside our normal capacity.

So our author seems to be saying that perfect virtue, whether humility or charity, is hardly attainable in this life. Human motives are inevitably always mixed, in the sense that we are never entirely free of egoism or self-will.

Perfect humility here on earth?

At the same time, with regard to humility, our author here makes a very interesting exception to this general rule. On some occasions, he writes, a soul may become so deeply engaged in contemplation and

> find its longing so heightened through the abundance of grace that, as often and as long as God deigns to bring it about, the soul will suddenly and completely lose and forget all knowledge and feeling of its existence, paying no attention to whether it has been holy or wretched . . . During this time, it is made perfectly humble, for it knows and feels no reason but the chief one [that is, the pure love for God].

He then adds, to make himself perfectly clear, that should such a person, in the course of their contemplation, become again aware of themselves, then they inevitably revert to being 'imperfectly humble'. In other words, once you again become self-conscious, aware of yourself as separate from God, you inevitably lose that quality of perfect humility. But, our author assures the reader, there is absolutely nothing wrong with that: 'It is good, all the same.'

What the *Cloud*-author is here referring to are those short-lived experiences of complete union with God, which may by the grace of God happen to contemplatives from time to time, yet only rarely and for a very short time.

So he follows this teaching up in the next chapter[8] by strongly denying that 'perfect humility' is necessary or even desirable in our present earthly life. We should aim always for 'imperfect humility', a true knowledge and awareness of ourselves as we really are. That is the vital and indispensable aim. So why does he teach about 'perfect humility' at all, as it is so rarely attainable? Because he wants his disciple to understand that contemplative prayer excels all other 'exercises, spiritual or bodily, that one can or may engage in by grace – how a secret thrust of love, directed in purity of spirit at this dark cloud of unknowing between you and your God, subtly and completely contains within it the perfect virtue of humility'.[9] In other words, the practice of contemplative prayer is the royal road to the grace of perfect humility, which while not fully attainable in this present life can at least be experienced in brief moments of ecstasy, as a foretaste of the condition of final bliss.

He then says, on a more personal note, 'I want you to know what perfect humility is, and to set it as a mark before the love of your heart, and to do this for yourself and for me; and because I want this knowledge to make you more humble.' So the vision of what is perfect humility is indispensable. Without such knowledge and awareness, 'foul and stinking pride' may creep in, and deceive us into imagining that we are becoming 'perfectly humble'. So our aim in this life has to be 'imperfect humility', but at the same time we are to remember that our ultimate goal is 'perfect humility'.

Charity

We turn now to the virtue of charity. Our author defines it thus: 'Charity means nothing but to love God for himself above all created things, and to love other human beings equally with yourself for God's sake.'[10] While his definition is clearly based on the twofold Gospel summary of the ancient Jewish law,[11] he puts it in such a way as to draw particular attention to the necessity of putting God 'above all created things'. Thus he reminds his readers of the central principle of the practice of contemplative prayer: it is the prayer that focuses on God alone while forgetting everything else in all creation, including all thoughts, images, hopes, fears and so on.

So he now makes the link between humility and charity in the context of contemplative prayer:

What has been said of humility – how it is subtly and completely contained within this little blind thrust of love when it is beating upon the dark cloud of unknowing with everything else thrust down and forgotten – should also be understood of all other virtues, and especially of charity.

The point is, as he reminds his readers, that the essence of contemplative prayer is 'nothing but a bare intention directed towards God himself', one in which, as he explains, there is no prayer (for example) 'for release from pain nor increase of reward, nor, in a word, anything but God himself'. It is therefore a prayer of complete self-abnegation, a prayer only that God's will may be done. So it is evident that 'in this work God is loved for himself and above all created things'. There can be no thought or recollection, he says, even of the most saintly person during this prayer of contemplation, nothing that would distract us from contemplating God himself.

Charity towards others

Our author then deals at more length with the relationship between contemplative prayer and charity towards other human beings, especially one's fellow Christians, which he calls 'the second or lower branch of charity'.[12] What he means by this is that love for God is prior to love for one's fellows in the sense that love for God has to be the mainspring and guiding light of love for human beings. As he himself puts it, 'charity means nothing but to love God for himself above all created things, and to love other human beings equally with yourself for God's sake.'[13]

The gift of contemplative prayer, he teaches, enables a person to develop an attitude of equal regard to everyone, whether the person he meets is a relative, a friend, a stranger, even a foe. 'For all alike seem kin to him, and none seems a stranger.' And he states this not as an ideal, but as something that 'appears from experience'. The implication of this observation is breathtakingly large. It seems that if *everyone* engaged in true contemplative prayer there would be no factions, no tribalism, no nationalism, no sexism, no racism, no divisions between human beings of any kind.

Two comments here, perhaps. We are reminded of the description of the almost idyllic common life of the first generation of Christians.[14] We may wonder whether this could be true in contemporary experience. My own personal encounters and experience of meeting regularly with others who practise contemplative prayer is that there is very often an extraordinary joyful unity that seems to transcend all the usual reserve that people have when they meet people who are otherwise unknown to them. We shall return to this shortly.[15]

The second point our author makes is that such all-embracing charity is never something we can make our aim in the actual exercise of contemplative prayer. This would defeat the purpose of focusing entirely on God. But he is sure that by means of praying in this way he will be made 'so virtuous and so charitable that afterwards', when he meets or prays for his fellow Christians, 'his will shall be as specifically directed to his foe as to his friend, to a stranger as to his kin, yes and sometimes more to his foe than to his friend'.[16] Again, we could refer to Jesus' teaching in the Sermon on the Mount: 'But I say to you, Love your enemies and pray for those who persecute you.'[17] The interesting point here is that our author turns what is a commandment of Jesus into a fruit of the work of the Spirit. As we shall see in the next chapter, this is typical of his spirituality. He is insistent that the practice of contemplative prayer liberates us from the oppressive feel of laws and commandments and moves us towards appreciating that virtues may be gained by strengthening the inner life of the spirit.

The third point he makes about charity is this. It may be a paradox, but treating everyone equally as a brother, sister or friend does not rule out close friendships with and affections for one, two or three particular people. Jesus himself had, he says, 'an intimate friendship for John, and for Mary,[18] and for Peter, more than many others'. There is a clear borderline between intimate friendship and preferential treatment. A good parent may like one child more than another, but he or she will not treat any of them unfairly.

Although he does not quote him directly, our author may have been acquainted with the writings of the Cistercian monk St Aelred of Rievaulx (1110–67), who wrote specifically about spiritual friendship. For Aelred, friendship is seen as one of the distinguishing marks of human beings, and he regarded the friendship of Christians as being of the highest order, because such friendship could bring about a profound unity of spirit.

Charity towards all humanity

Finally, in a most moving and visionary paragraph,[19] our author bids his disciple remember that just as

> all men were lost with Adam, and all men who bear witness in
> their works to their desire for salvation are and will be saved by

sole virtue of Christ's Passion, so – not in the same way, yet as it were in the same way – a soul that is perfectly disposed to this work and thus united with God in spirit, as experience of this work reveals, does all that it can to make all men as perfect in this work as it is itself.

In other words, anyone who is called to contemplative prayer will find in their own experience of such prayer that they cannot escape God's call to do their utmost to attract and draw as many of their fellow human beings as possible into this same way of prayer. For Christ came to save not a few select people but the whole of humanity by his Passion. All of us who are Christian people have not an identical role, it is true, but a similar and subsidiary part in enabling all who seek salvation to discover how they can be united with God in contemplative prayer here and now. Making little distinction here between humanity as a whole and the Church,[20] he draws on St Paul's well-known teaching of the analogy between the Church and the human body.[21] He underlines the interconnectedness of all its members. Charity demands that:

anyone who wishes to be a perfect disciple of our Lord needs to stretch up his spirit in this work for the salvation of all his brothers and sisters in nature, as our Lord stretched out his body on the cross. And how? Not for his friends and kin, and those he loves most intimately, but for all humanity, without special regard to one rather than another. For all who desire to give up sin and ask for mercy will be saved by virtue of Christ's Passion.

Anyone who thinks that the contemplative way of prayer is only for a specialist elite or for the introverted needs to think again. It is a prayer that leads to expansion of the spirit, and the opening up of new and refreshing horizons.

6

Sin and the self

———•◆•———

Sin – *The Cloud*: chapters 2, 4, 10–12, 15,
16, 27, 28, 33, 36, 40, 59
The self – *The Cloud*: chapters 13, 14, 30, 44, 45, 65–68

For most modern Western people, sin is not quite the problem it
was for our ancestors. It is perfectly true that in our public worship
we regularly confess our sins, and some make use of the sacrament
of Confession. On the other hand, as recently suggested by an experienced priest and spiritual teacher, Angela Tilby, for many people
today sin is not something that concerns them much. It is not that
sin has gone away or that people are not concerned about right
and wrong, or good and evil: far from it. Nor is it true that people
are no longer capable of self-examination or self-criticism. It is just
that many people find it hard to come to grips with the *idea* of sin,
whether personal or corporate. Tilby writes:

> People go through the motions, but it is not always clear that
> either the heart or the brain is engaged. Meanwhile the unease and
> guilt which we habitually carry around with us finds no expres-
> sion and no relief. The consequence of this is that people . . .
> tend to take their real concerns elsewhere and not bring them
> to church. *Feelings*, say, of guilt, or worthlessness; *problems*, such
> as compulsive behaviour; *disordered thoughts* of limitless power
> or revenge tend to be endured in silence or shared, if at all, with
> a therapist or counsellor.[1]

Whether or not we agree with her assessment, it is certainly the case
that if people think seriously about sin at all, they understand it as

45

breaking the rules or as injustice rather than as something universal expressing the gap between the Holy God and fallen humanity.

Until relatively recent times, the Christian mindset was very different. For the *Cloud*-author, and his contemporaries, sin was an unavoidable reality and the greatest obstacle to be overcome if people are to find both peace of mind and lasting happiness. Actual sins, whether of thought, word or deed, are symptoms of human sinfulness, which in turn arises from original sin – the innate human tendency, inherited from Adam and Eve, to choose evil rather than good, wrong rather than right. As we might put it today, sinfulness is in our genes. For him, as indeed for almost all teachers in the Christian tradition until recent times, sin is characteristic of the normal human condition. Its most common manifestation can be observed in self-centred pride, which causes people to dethrone God and enthrone themselves in the centre of their world.

But sin has many faces. Our author refers to the traditional distinction between capital or grievous sins, which cut us off completely from God, and venial or less serious sins, which can become serious if allowed to become habitual. He also refers to the traditional list of seven deadly sins: pride, anger, envy, covetousness, sloth, gluttony and lust. These again can be venial or grievous.

Although he certainly takes sin seriously, the *Cloud*-author, like all good spiritual directors, treats it in a balanced manner. He avoids both what today might be described as excessive moralism on the one hand, and permissive relativism on the other. As was shrewdly observed by someone of my acquaintance, there are remarkably few 'shoulds' and 'shouldn'ts' in his book. The subject of sin is very much secondary to his primary theme: how we human beings can grow into unity with God.

His teaching is set out and expressed most clearly and attractively in the middle of the book. He puts it like this:

Fill your spirit with the spiritual import of the word SIN, without specific regard to the type of sin, whether it is venial or mortal . . . What need is there for contemplatives to care what or how great a sin it is? To them all sins seem equally great – I mean during this work of contemplation – when the smallest sin separates them from God and holds them back from spiritual peace.[2]

The lump of sin

We then come to one of our author's most memorable pieces of advice: to 'feel sin as a lump, you do not know what, but nothing other than yourself. And then shout continuously in spirit "sin, sin, sin! out, out, out".' He continues: 'This spiritual shout is better learned from God by experience than from any human being by word.'

Before commenting on his suggested practice of shouting 'in spirit . . . sin, sin, sin', we need to get a clearer picture of what he means by 'sin, coagulated into a lump, which is nothing other than yourself'. This is exactly the phrase he uses a few chapters earlier when he is commending to contemplatives the practice of reflective meditation on the goodness of God or on their own sinfulness. He urges his readers not to try to analyse or interpret these words [God or sin], 'as if by so doing you wanted to heighten your devotion', but simply 'to keep these words completely whole and focus on sin as a lump, you do not know what, nothing other than yourself'.[3]

By describing sin as a lump, he is describing something of its unattractive nature – an unwanted growth, a shapeless mess, an intrusion. In the interests of honesty and truth, when we confess our sins we need to be precise, not vague, to make a clean breast of them, as we say; but once we have expressed our sorrow sincerely, and made a genuine purpose of amendment, we need to put them right behind us, and certainly not get obsessed with our particular shortcomings, but constantly recall God's love and grace. Once again, we come back to his fundamental and essential principle. No amount of *thinking* about God, or about the *nature of sin*, can bring us one inch nearer God. Only the exercise of offering a humble stirring of love to God can break through the barrier of the cloud of unknowing. *God cannot be grasped by thought, only by love.*

The most eloquent illustration of his teaching is to be found in his earlier description of Mary Magdalene's spiritual transformation.[4]

When our Lord said to Mary, as the representative of all sinners who are called to the contemplative life, 'Thy sins are forgiven thee', it was not because of her great sorrow, nor because of her consciousness of her sins, nor again because of the humility which arose merely from the consideration of her sinfulness. Why then? Because she loved greatly.[5]

He continues:

Though she could not cease to feel deep heartfelt sorrow for her sins . . . nevertheless it may be said . . . that she had a more heartfelt sorrow and a more grievous desire, and she sighed more deeply and pined more painfully, yes, almost to the death, for lack of love (although she had abundance of love) than she did for any consciousness of sins. And do not marvel at this, for it is the nature of a true lover that the more he loves, the more he longs for to love.

The key to the lock that must be opened is not sorrow for our sins, however grievous they may have been, but rather love, or rather sorrow for our *lack* of love.

The appeal he makes is to our human experience of loving. The true lover, no matter how much he or she loves another, always longs to love his or her beloved more. Mary's sins, she knew, 'were what had divided her from her God whom she loved so much and also they were in large part the reason why she pined in sickness for lack of love'. But then he asks the question:

But what of that? Did she come down from the height of desire, [that is for God] into the depth of her sinful life and search in the foul stinking fen and dunghill of her sins, sorting them one by one in every detail, and sorrowing and weeping for each of them separately? No, certainly, she did not.

Here he puts his finger on the futility and absurdity of getting 'bogged down' in analysing one's sins and shortcomings. By the gift of God's inward grace Mary knew very well that if she went down that road, she would never succeed in attaining to union with God. With shrewd psychological understanding he adds, 'For in that way she was more likely to have aroused in herself the possibility of sinning again than to have obtained complete forgiveness of all her sins.' It is not unlike people who embark on a slimming regime to reduce their weight. Often going on a controlled diet has the effect of making them more conscious of food. Then, as the temptations to break their diet regime seem to become more irresistible, they are more liable to fail in their objective. So too, dwelling on our sins is counter-productive. Indulging in such reflections simply opens ourselves up to further temptations.

Turning now to the earlier discussion in this section, what are we to make of the advice to 'shout continuously in spirit "sin, sin, sin! out, out, out"'? His advice here may strike us as rather unorthodox, because he seems to suggest that sin, which he has just described as 'nothing other than yourself', can be driven out by force of will, by raising the volume of our silent internal voice. But, of course, as Paul made clear, sin is stubbornly resistant to the human will. 'I can will what is right, but I cannot do it.'[6] However, we need to interpret his advice in the context of his explanation of how we access God by the 'one little word', which he gave a couple of pages before, and which we have already discussed.[7]

Just as when we approach God by putting on one side all thoughts about God's works and concentrate all our mental and spiritual energy into saying our one word (for example, 'love' or 'God'), so we are to put aside all thoughts and memories of our sins, and simply focus on the one word 'sin': 'this foul, stinking lump of sin, as it were united and coagulated into the substance of your being'. He implies that his advice comes not from any textbook, but from his own personal experience. He seems to be referring to an experi-ence that has touched him externally and physically just as much as interiorly and spiritually, bringing him to a deeper depth of humility and sorrow for his sinfulness. How far we may use or adapt this particular advice of his I am not sure. As far as I am aware, no contemporary teacher uses it. Maybe its usefulness to us will depend, as it did for the *Cloud*-author, upon our own particular personal experience.

There is another question arising from this section still to be discussed – the question of how far sin is, as he writes, so inseparable from oneself that it is 'as it were united and coagulated into the sub-stance of your being'. We shall come back to this later in this chapter when we discuss the self.

Dealing with the root and ground of sin

Now we come to our author's most penetrating and liberating message. He is convinced that contemplative prayer 'is the only work that by itself destroys the root and ground of sin'.[8] He declares that no matter how austere a lifestyle you take up, 'however much you fasted, however long you stayed awake, however early you rose, however hard the bed you lay on, however harsh the garment you wore', and so on, such self-sacrifices will never bring you into union with God. And the same goes even for your devotions centred, say, on Christ's Passion, good and beneficial though they may be.

There is one thing and one thing only that brings you into unity with God and that is this 'blind movement of love'. 'Without this these things bring little or no benefit. It [such an impulse of love] not only destroys the ground and root of sin, so far as is possible on earth, it also brings virtues.'

Behind this radical teaching of the *Cloud*-author we surely hear echoes of the most famous passage St Paul ever wrote – the hymn to love, in which we read the words: 'If I hand over my body so that I may boast, but do not have love, I gain nothing.'[9] St Paul means that if, in wishing to witness to Christ, I give myself up to the most painful of deaths, but have no love, even this brings no credit to me. Love alone has the power to open up ourselves to God and to others. As the distinguished Bible scholar Charles Barrett writes: 'Love is the indispensable addition which gives worth to all other Christian gifts.'[10]

As the *Cloud*-author argues, it is this blind impulse of love towards God in the cloud of unknowing that opens us up to the real possibility of union with God. This in turn leads us into a life on earth in which it becomes possible that by the grace of God the virtues of humility and charity may come to be practised. A health-giving relationship to God bears the fruit of health-giving relationships with our fellow human beings. In contemplative prayer God works through us and in us to bring healing to our fragmented, sick and damaged selves. God alone can get to the root and ground of the problem of sin.

The self

The *Cloud*-author is a complete realist. He has no illusions about the dangers of self-deception. 'I tell you truly that the Devil has his contemplatives even as God has his.'[11] He is particularly concerned for young men and women. He believes that they are prone to strain themselves physically, emotionally and spiritually, by applying the teaching in a superficial, physical or overexcited way. So like St Benedict, and all good spiritual directors, he is at pains to stress the importance of a balanced lifestyle in which the body is given its proper place. Eating, drinking, sleeping, clothing yourself against extreme cold or heat, how long you pray or read for, how much time you spend in conversation – all are matters that require self-management and self-discipline. The watchword here is moderation.[12]

> For the love of God, guard against sickness as much as you reasonably can, so that you are not the cause of your own sickness. For I tell you truly that this work [of contemplative prayer] demands the greatest tranquillity, and a state of health and purity in body as much as in soul.[13]

He also advises: 'But if sickness comes . . . have patience and humbly await God's mercy, and then all will be well enough.'

Yet about one thing he counsels that there can be no moderation, and that is in the actual work of contemplative prayer. In other words, if we are serious in our intention, we need to make this work of contemplation our absolute top priority. Then all else in our lives will fall into its proper place. We are reminded of Jesus' teaching: 'Strive first for the kingdom of God and his righteousness, and all these things will be given to you as well.'[14] Once again he reiterates: 'So lift up your heart with a blind stirring of love . . . God wants you.'[15]

Spiritual sorrow

In the following two chapters[16] the *Cloud*-author explores what he calls 'a deep and powerful spiritual sorrow' which comes from 'the naked knowledge and feeling of your own existence'. What does he mean by this? He has already taught the need for the contemplative

51

to 'overthrow all knowledge and feeling of anything below God, and of trampling it all down deep beneath the cloud of forgetting'. He now returns to this point, emphasizing the further necessity of forgetting both yourself and your actions for God's sake, making yourself as it were nothing: 'For it is the nature of a perfect lover not only to love more than himself the thing that he loves but also in a sense to hate himself for the sake of the thing he loves.'

Our author is appealing here again to the self-disciplined character of human loving, in which the beloved and his or her needs are given preference over the lover's own needs.

Our author has yet something further to say about the psychological and spiritual journey taken in contemplative prayer.

When you have forgotten all other created things and all that you yourself do, there will still remain, between you and your God . . . a naked knowledge and feeling of your own existence, and that knowledge and feeling always need to be destroyed, before it comes about that you can truly experience perfect contemplation.

What is he saying here? First of all, he goes on to explain that this self-awareness 'cannot be destroyed without a special grace freely given by God, together with a corresponding capacity on your part to receive that grace'. And 'this capacity', he says, 'is nothing but a deep and powerful spiritual sorrow'.[17]

The important point he is making here is that to feel *what* one is – that is, one's individual nature and personality – is one thing, but to feel *that* one is has to be quite another and more fundamental thing: to be aware of the very fact of one's existence.[18] This feeling, he says, is so terribly painful that compared with other sorrows it is overwhelming, and only bearable because of the delight experienced in contemplative prayer, and because it is bound up with the desire to be united with God.

What does he mean, then, by this profound sorrow? It seems to arise from the conscious awareness of one's essential separation from God, a separation which it is almost impossible to overcome, and yet which we desire so much to overcome. It is a little like (though not the same as) the sorrow of a deeply loving man and his partner who become aware that they cannot ever be entirely and utterly united with each other. There is no problem with their mutual bond. It could hardly be stronger. But nevertheless at a profound level there is always going to be some sense of separation, a cause of inner anguish that they are not one, but always and inevitably different.

The *Cloud*-author's conviction is that 'every soul needs to experience and feel within itself this sorrow and this desire . . . until the time comes when they can be perfectly united to God in perfect charity'.[19]

Self-transcendence

The *Cloud*-author has something else important to say about the relationship between the contemplative person and the self.

Contemplative prayer is not about enjoying ecstasies, levitations, hearing voices, seeing visions, or any kind of out-of-body or psycho-somatic experiences. Contemplative prayer takes place interiorly, silently in the spirit, and is best practised with the body entirely still. 'Take great care, then, that your spiritual work is nowhere in the body.' If you focus your mind on any material object, whatever it is, you can be certain that you will be there in spirit, and therefore not engaged in contemplation. From the point of view of the body, as it were, when a person is engaged in contemplative prayer nothing, absolutely nothing, is happening. So to the physical senses, 'it seems as if you are doing nothing'. But the reality is that you are 'working away at this nothing. So do not give up, but labour eagerly in that nothing with an unsleeping desire, longing to have God, whom no one can know.'[20]

He continues in the same vein:[21]

This nothing can be better felt than seen, for it is quite obscure and quite dark to those who have only been looking at it for a short time; yet to put it more accurately, in experiencing it a soul is blinded by abundance of spiritual light more than by darkness or lack of bodily light.

As the *Cloud*-author continues this discussion, for the first and only time he quotes St Denis the Areopagite, the main influence behind his own teaching.[22] He does so hesitantly, he writes, as he is aware that authorities are quoted by some writers because they wish to appear learned or clever. That is not his intention; he wishes only to refer his readers to the teacher whom he holds in high regard, and indeed one of whose books he translated.[23]

Physical and spiritual transformation

Finally, our author has one other quite startling thing to say about the effects of contemplative prayer: 'The work of contemplation will have a favourable effect on the body as well as the soul of anyone who practises it, and make him agreeable to everyone, man or woman, who sees him.'[24] So much so that the least handsome or beautiful person would be 'suddenly transformed into graciousness', and 'Thus all good people who saw them would be glad and joyful to have their company, and would find that in their presence they were very greatly comforted in spirit and helped by grace towards God.' He goes on to claim that contemplatives would be well able to judge people of all kinds and characters, and also to adapt themselves to all they meet: 'to the amazement of all who saw him, drawing others by the help of grace to the same spiritual work that he himself practises'.

Genuinely contemplative people become physically attractive, a pleasure to know, their company is enjoyable, and they have the power to draw others towards the same way of prayer.

7

Christis and The Cloud

------◆●◆------

The Cloud of Unknowing, as was remarked in the Introduction, has a contemporary appeal to a significant number of people who may count themselves outside or on the fringe of the Church. But this wider appeal in turn may raise questions for some of those who think of themselves as within the mainstream of Christian belief. The questions they may ask are these. Can we discern in our author's teaching a line that is consistent with the teaching and practice of Jesus himself? Can we recognize in his book the Jesus Christ we know from the New Testament, who is both fully human and fully divine? How far does the author value the work of the Holy Spirit? Is the God of its author the same God the Holy Trinity, Father, Son and Holy Spirit, as understood by the Church through the ages?

First, it may be helpful here to say a word about the *Cloud*-author's method and style of writing. As has already been pointed out,[1] he doesn't usually quote directly either from Holy Scripture or from Church authorities. As he says, he rather wishes to be heard by 'those who have ears to hear' – that is, by those who are prepared to listen to him as one who is speaking from his own experience of contemplative prayer. But having said that, it is evident to the reader that his book reveals the author as someone who is utterly steeped both in the Scriptures and in the Church Fathers. There are up to 300 scriptural quotations, and dozens from later Church authorities.

Central to his theological outlook is his conviction that we desire God because God first desires us.[2] It is the outstanding beauty, both moral and physical, of the human personality of Jesus Christ that attracts people to follow him, and yes, the moral and even visible beauty of Jesus' true followers that in turn attract others.[3] A brief look

at the Gospels reveals much that may resonate with the teaching of
The Cloud.

Jesus' teaching and practice of prayer

Let's start with the Sermon on the Mount. Here the first point Jesus
makes to his followers is to avoid the kind of egoistic self-display that
leads to hypocrisy. He advises his disciples to go into 'your [inner or
secret] room and shut the door and pray to your Father who is in
secret'.[4] This inner or secret room would have been a store room with
no windows – a suitable place for anyone who wished to avoid being
seen by others. The essential point is that it is a place that is hidden
away. So the only witness of a disciple's prayer is God himself. However,
the fourth-century monk John Cassian, who learned his practice
of prayer from the Desert Fathers, believed that this instruction has
an alternative or metaphorical meaning. Not everyone lives in a house
with an inner room. But wherever anyone is, whether in a house,
or a cave, or a cell, or in the open air, he or she can pray in their heart
(inner room), with their lips closed (door shut). This symbolic
interpretation of Jesus' words became widely accepted through later
centuries in monastic communities, and now often also informs contemporary teaching about contemplative prayer.

The second point Jesus makes is the advice to pray with few words.
'Do not heap up empty phrases as the Gentiles do; for they think that
they will be heard because of their many words. Do not be like them,
for your Father knows what you need before you ask him.' We have
already commented on our author's conviction that 'short prayers
pierce heaven',[5] a well-known saying found in a number of writings
of the early Fathers of the Church, and particularly appropriate as a
basis both for so-called arrow prayers and for contemplative prayer.
The saying may not have its actual origin in Jesus' teaching, but it is
obviously agreeable to it. There could not be a shorter, less wordy
prayer than the prayer of 'one little word' which the contemplative is
recommended to use by our author.

The 'Lord's Prayer' itself is the third strand of Jesus' teaching in
the Sermon on the Mount. Although this prayer very soon became
a regular formula in the worship of the Church, its original purpose

is likely to have been quite closely related to Jesus' teaching about the kingdom and his own mission. It reflects his overall aim to call people to acknowledge and expect a new world in which God's sovereignty, kingdom and purpose are paramount, and our own human needs for forgiveness, daily bread and protection are to be seen as arising from that. So the twofold theme of 'Love God, love your neighbour' is the moral and theological foundation of the Lord's Prayer. And here we may recall our author's teaching that contemplative prayer expresses charity towards God, charity towards others, charity towards all humanity.[6] So there is a clear connection.

Jesus' teaching in Matthew 6 is by no means the sum total of his teaching on prayer. By using parables, and also more directly, he teaches the absolute necessity of faith, fidelity, perseverance, boldness, and of seeking first the kingdom of God, and God's righteousness. Above all, he teaches a relationship to God that is modelled on our less than perfect relationship to our own earthly fathers, but one that also transcends such human relationships.

Like all the best teachers, however, Jesus taught as much by example as he did by word. And surely the most striking thing about his own practice was his frequent withdrawals to the hills and deserted places of Galilee, where he would spend whole nights in prayer. How Jesus prayed when he was alone on these occasions we cannot, of course, know because there was no one to witness it.[7] The nature and context of these solitary times of withdrawal, however, is certainly consistent with the possibility that the form of prayer he used was that of a contemplative. It was likely to be a prayer in which he focused his loving attention on his heavenly Father. In this time of prayer he would not have been troubled by the awareness of his own sin, for he was, as Scripture testifies,[8] without sin. But he would surely have been aware of his human weakness and mortality, as on occasions he certainly experienced weariness, hunger and thirst. Thus he was in a spiritual condition of perfect humility.[9]

Following the line of the *Cloud*-author's exposition of the nature of Mary of Bethany's prayer, discussed in an earlier chapter,[10] we might come to ask this question. Could there not be a hint there of what may have been Christ's own prayer, one of absolute attention to the Father, a total offering himself in love to the Father in 'the cloud of unknowing', in which all the distractions of an exhausting life of teaching and healing are cast down into the cloud of forgetting? The *Cloud*-author makes no such claim, for it would be a step too far into speculation. But it is surely worth asking the question.[11]

Letting go of our images of Christ

One of the most seductive dangers for all religious people is that of having a false or partial image of God, and, so far as Christians are concerned, equally a false image of Christ. The most obvious example we have in the New Testament of someone whose love for Jesus was second to none is St Paul. He is acutely aware of the danger of a mistaken image of him.

Of his total devotion to Christ he writes, for example, 'for to me, living is Christ . . . my desire is to depart [this life] and be with Christ, for that is far better'.[12] Later he goes on to add: 'For [Christ's] sake I have suffered the loss of all things, and I regard them as rubbish, in order that I may gain Christ and be found in him.'[13]

On the other hand, Paul also writes: 'From now on, therefore, we regard no one from a human point of view [literally, according to the flesh]; even though we once knew Christ from a human point of view [literally, according to the flesh], we know him no longer in that way.'[14] The meaning of the second half of this sentence is disputed, but the most probable one is this: 'Don't make the Messiah (Christ) in your own human image.'[15] This is exactly the mistake that Peter made following his confession of faith at Caesarea Philippi, when he was severely rebuked by Jesus for his refusal to accept that Jesus' destiny was to be that of a suffering Messiah.[16]

It is also, of course, notoriously the same mistake that Saul of Tarsus (later to become known as Paul) had himself once made. In his youth Saul (Paul) believed that the Messiah, when he came, would be one who would rigorously uphold the Law of Moses and come down in wrath and judgement against all who were disobedient to it. But then, through his conversion, arising from his direct encounter with the risen Christ outside Damascus, he came to see that to make God the object of a longing for an exclusive kingdom was a terrible danger for Jews and Christians alike. It is hardly necessary to refer here to the dangers of intolerant exclusivity of any kind in the world today. Do not make the Messiah in your own image. Do not make your God in your own image.

This danger of making Jesus in our own image does not mean that we should turn away from reflecting on the character and mission of Jesus as we know them from the Gospels. Christ's life, ministry, Passion, death and resurrection are at the heart of our knowledge of the God who revealed himself in Jesus Christ. The *Cloud*-author would absolutely agree with that. The reading of Scripture, hearing teaching based on Scripture, *lectio divina* and reflection on Scripture are part of the necessary preparation that any contemplative must make, and is exactly what he commends. Throughout his book, however, the point he is repeatedly making is that *in the actual work of contemplative prayer* we have to let go of all our knowledge, reflection, and images of Christ and of God – in his words, 'to trample them down into the cloud of forgetting' – in order to give our total attention to God in Christ. God may be approached by thought but no one can arrive at union with God by intellectual effort. Only by love, by darts of longing love, may God be grasped. All our images of Christ and of God, however good, must therefore be put aside during the actual work of contemplative prayer.

God in Christ, creator and redeemer

God's work in creating and redeeming humankind is at the heart of the teaching of *The Cloud*. Thus he writes in the first chapter: 'God, in the everlasting love by which he made and fashioned you . . . and then redeemed you at the cost of his precious blood when you were lost in Adam.'[17] And he often repeats the need to prepare for contemplative prayer by recollecting and meditating on Christ's Incarnation and Passion, and by having compassion for Christ in his Passion.[18] Echoing St Paul, he also reminds his readers that 'all men were lost with Adam, and all men who bear witness in their works to their desire for salvation are and will be saved by sole virtue of Christ's Passion'.[19] Christ is our Saviour. There is no other way to salvation other than trusting the good news that Jesus Christ has saved us by suffering and dying on the cross.

One element of Christ's saving work that he hardly mentions, however, is the resurrection. It may come as a surprise to readers that for many centuries in Western Christianity the resurrection of Christ, although of course central to Christian belief, was not seen as a significant part of God's saving work in Christ, and therefore not universally referred to in the Eucharist.[20]

Jesus Christ, God and man

On the issue of Jesus Christ's humanity and divinity, the *Cloud*-author bats straight down the middle of the wicket. He virtually never mentions Christ's divinity without reference to his humanity, and vice versa.

We see this very early on in his book, where we find some interesting teaching about the use and misuse of time. The author here imagines a dialogue between his novice and himself, in which the novice wonders how he will cope with the time demands of his contemplative work. The author then speaks of his own sense of weakness and inability to cope. The novice cries out in response: 'Help me now for the love of Jesus!', to which our author responds:

> You did well to say, 'For the love of Jesus', for in the love of Jesus shall be your help. Love is so great a power that it makes all possessions common. Love Jesus, therefore, and all he has is yours. As God he is the maker and giver of time; as Man he is the true governor of time; and as God and Man together he is the truest judge and auditor of time.[21]

This is a fascinating insight. As A. C. Spearing points out, the *Cloud*-author here reveals a down-to-earth acquaintance with the language of commerce and accountancy, such as partnership, profit, auditing and so on.[22] This is to highlight the fact that there is a kind of universal economy of love. Out of his love for us, God the Creator in Christ supplies us with the gift of time in abundance, while it is equally true that Jesus the Man, who is our brother and partner, guides and keeps us in the proper use of time and enables us to be profitable servants.

There are many other examples of how the *Cloud*-author weaves together his understanding of and love for Christ, in both his humanity and his divinity. In an earlier chapter we saw how Mary of Bethany listened to Jesus' human words, but saw beyond them to his divinity 'as she hung her love and her longing desire on this cloud of unknowing'.[23] Our author acknowledges 'the excellence of his blessed body ... and the sweet voice and words belonging to his Manhood' but then points out that 'she attended only to the supreme wisdom of his Godhead cloaked within the dark words of his Manhood – to that she attended with all the love of her heart'. As one thirteenth-century French mystic said:

> Just as in the first degree [of contemplation] the devoted soul gazes upon the man rather than God ... [in the final stage] the object of his contemplation must be the Godhead rather than the humanity. He must take hold of God by the handle of his humanity and embrace rather the feet of God.[24]

Or, to put it very simply, as the contemplative deepens his attention on Jesus he or she sees through the veil of his humanity to adore his divinity.

Another illustration of the *Cloud*-author's sure touch is the commentary he offers on the Ascension of our Lord, and on the visions of St Stephen the first martyr and St Martin of Tours. In this section of his book he is concerned with those who misunderstand the nature of contemplative prayer by taking in a literal way language about 'looking up to God'.[25] After referring to Jesus' bodily Ascension into heaven[26] he asks the question, 'Does that mean that when contemplating we should always stare upwards with our eyes, to look whether we can see him sitting or standing bodily in heaven, as St Stephen did?' Of course not, he answers. We have no idea of the nature of Jesus' physical existence in heaven:

> How his body is in heaven, standing, sitting, or lying, no one knows, and there is no need for it to be known, or to know anything more than that his body was raised up with his soul, without separation. The body and soul, which are his Manhood, are united with his Godhead, also without separation.

If the risen and ascended Lord does appear to anyone on earth, as he did to Stephen at his death (and famously to Paul on his way to

Damascus), he will do so where he pleases to be, with the bodily form that is most suitable, and one that signals some appropriate spiritual significance.

Mystical experiences

Even if he does not put it quite like that, St Paul surely understood this very well. What he does tell us is this:

> I know a person in Christ who fourteen years ago was caught up to the third heaven – whether in the body or out of the body I do not know; God knows . . . was caught up into Paradise and heard things that are not to be told, that no mortal is permitted to repeat.[27]

From the context there seems no doubt at all that Paul is referring to a personal experience of his own. But he is reluctant to claim it as his own, and that's why he does not speak of this experience in the first person, as that could seem like boasting. He says rather he will boast only of his weaknesses. It is clear that this was what today we would call a mystical experience. The interesting thing is that Paul, although he obviously valued this experience – or he would not have mentioned it – makes so little of it, by admitting that it only happened once, some 14 years before. We notice that the details of this unusual event do not concern him: whether, for example, it was purely spiritual or, as we would describe it today, psychosomatic (both physical and spiritual). The *Cloud*-author similarly downplays mystical experiences, however exciting, as irrelevant and for the most part unprofitable for the work of contemplative prayer.[28] We can therefore be clear that neither St Paul nor he put much value on such transitory events.

And now we come to our final two questions. Does the *Cloud*-author take seriously the work of the Holy Spirit? And how does his teaching square with the Church's teaching on the nature of God the Holy Trinity?

The Holy Spirit and the Trinity

A contemporary reader might notice how little the *Cloud*-author seems to refer to the work of the Holy Spirit. He does mention more than once the Holy Spirit's guidance,[29] but he also warns of the danger of confusing the fire of love that is kindled by the Holy Spirit with the unnatural self-induced fervour of false contemplatives.[30] At all times, as a good spiritual director, the *Cloud*-author is concerned with the importance of discerning the gifts of the Spirit. And it seems likely that he was especially anxious about the misunderstandings that could arise from the teachings of some of his contemporaries. Richard Rolle in particular could be read as placing greater value on what today would be called charismatic or mystical experiences of a sensational character. The *Cloud*-author plays down such experiences, and we may feel that he is wise to do so, bearing in mind how easily people get carried away and dangerously excited by external phenomena.

The second point to bear in mind is that when our author uses the word 'spiritual', which he does more often than he refers to the Holy Spirit, he means a quality or an activity within the human soul that is much more specific than would be the case with most modern writers. In fact he is always referring to the work of the Holy Spirit within the human spirit.

The Cloud is essentially a handbook for practitioners rather than a catechism. Perhaps, therefore, we should not be too concerned that the author has nothing to say about God as Holy Trinity.[31] It would be difficult to disagree with the judgement of James Walsh, who simply comments that 'the Deity whom the author is addressing is . . . the God, one and three, of Christian revelation'.[32]

8

Contemporary teaching and practice

During the last 30 or so years there has been a wonderful flowering of movements teaching the practice of contemplative prayer. Two of the largest and most widespread of these, Centering Prayer and Christian Meditation, have drawn much of their teaching and practice from *The Cloud of Unknowing*. This is clear evidence of just how much influence this book has had some seven centuries after it was written.

Centering Prayer

The Centering Prayer movement began in the mid-1970s, at a time of turbulent change in the Roman Catholic Church following the Second Vatican Council. At the same time, there was an exodus of young Westerners looking to the East for a new spirituality. Thomas Keating, the Abbot of St Joseph's Abbey in Massachusetts, challenged his brother Cistercian monks: 'Is it not possible to put the essence of the Christian contemplative tradition in a format accessible to modern men and women?'

The practice of Transcendental Meditation was making inroads in the USA, and many of the monks were themselves beginning to study it. In looking for a model – an outer form of sitting meditation based on a faithful reproduction of the Christian understanding of contemplative prayer – one of the monks, William Meninger, instinctively went to *The Cloud* for guidance. Meninger had been reading and constantly rereading *The Cloud of Unknowing* until it had become deeply rooted in him. He knew exactly what he was looking for in chapter 7: 'If you want to have this (naked) intention (directed towards God) wrapped and enfolded in one word, so that you can hold on to it better, take only a short word of one syllable.' From this Meninger developed the basic practice of sitting meditation. Keating and another monk, Basil Pennington, both brilliant communicators, helped to refine and promulgate it.

They quickly adopted the term 'Centering Prayer', using a phrase of Thomas Merton (1915–68): 'The best way to come to God is go to your own centre and pass through the centre into the centre of God.'[1] The instructions given to those who wish to practise Centering Prayer may be summed up as follows.

First, sit down on a chair or a prayer stool. Keep your body relaxed but alert. Your aim is to be totally open to God, all the way down to that innermost point of your being, deeper than your thinking, deeper than your feelings, memories or desires, deeper than your usual sense of yourself. This corresponds to what *The Cloud* calls a 'naked intent direct to God', and is the essence of Centering Prayer. Then choose a sacred word or phrase, which is a symbol of your willingness to carry out this intention. This could be 'Jesus', 'Father', 'Abba' or a word expressing your attitude, such as 'open', 'still', 'listen'. This word or short phrase is not a mantra to be repeated constantly, but a word that is said silently and interiorly which you use only when you notice you have been distracted. This sacred word corresponds to the 'one little word' of *The Cloud*. While meditating you must not change your word, but stick to the one you have chosen. Meditate for a minimum of 20 minutes.

Do not look for the fruits of meditation in your subjective experience of it. Centering Prayer, like the prayer of *The Cloud*, is not about accessing sublime states of consciousness or having mystical experiences. The fruits are to be seen in daily life, in greater patience, more willingness to forgive and greater honesty in your own being.

The aim of this method is thus very simple. It is to prepare the mind and heart for the gift of contemplative prayer, which can only come as a gift of God's grace. And the essence of it is entering into, and keeping, the intention to be open to God.

It is not only for full-time contemplatives, such as the *Cloud*-author was writing for, but primarily for those who are active in the world: lay people, priests and ministers as well as members of religious communities. The movement has made astonishingly rapid progress, attracting people not only in the United States but in over 30 countries in all continents. Many books have been written about it, and workshops and retreats held in many centres across the world.

Today there are a number of different 'schools' teaching Centering Prayer. The dominant school is called Contemplative Outreach, of which Thomas Keating is the founder. On its website you will find the mission statement:

Contemplative Outreach is a spiritual network of individuals and small faith communities committed to living the contemplative dimension of the Gospel in everyday life through the practice of Centering Prayer. The contemplative dimension of the Gospel manifests itself in an ever deepening union with the living Christ and the practical caring for others that flows from that relationship.

Thus the Contemplative Outreach movement highlights not only a commitment to the interior practice of seeking union with Christ through silence and stillness, but also draws attention to the call to live a contemplative life within a faith community – a community in which the Gospel imperative of practical caring for others is also central. As we have already commented,[2] the *Cloud*-author has his own perspective on the relationship between these different aspects of the Christian life. He gives the contemplative vocation a higher status than that of the active. Yet he is also perfectly clear that a calling to the contemplative life is not possible without prior active commitment to 'good and honourable corporal works of mercy and charity'.[3] The Centering Prayer movement thus builds on and extends the teaching of *The Cloud*, and makes it explicit that contemplation cannot be divorced from social action.

Christian Meditation

At much the same time as the Centering Prayer movement was beginning, the Benedictine monk John Main (1926–82) began to teach a similar practice at Ealing Abbey in London. He called it 'Christian Meditation'. Some 20 years earlier, while working as a layman and diplomat in Malaysia, he had learned from an Indian teacher how the

Hindu tradition of meditation, using a silent prayer word or mantra, could be adapted to his Christian faith. However, when he returned to Britain and entered Ealing Abbey as a novice monk, he was forbidden to pray in this way. It was not until 1970, as headmaster of a Catholic secondary school in Washington DC, that he found what he was looking for in the fourth-century monk John Cassian.

Cassian had imbibed the teaching of the desert monks, whose example and teaching had been such a powerful inspiration to the Church. They were struggling to come to terms with the fact that after almost three hundred years of state persecution the Christian faith had overnight, under the Emperor Constantine, become the official religion of the Roman Empire. The downside of now being part of the imperial Establishment was the serious dilution of a personal and committed spirituality in the Church. It was the monks who kept this flame alive for the wider Church. Cassian himself influenced St Benedict (*c*.480–550), and Benedict's Rule of Life for monks has continued to be a resource and inspiration for an interior spirituality in the Western Church – not just within the Benedictine orders but throughout virtually all religious communities.

In Cassian's teaching on prayer,[4] John Main believed that he had found a Christian foundation for the practice of silent, contemplative prayer, in particular the repetition of a short phrase or prayer word in order to keep the attention focused on God. He wrote:

> Cassian recommended anyone who wanted to learn to pray continually to take a single short verse and to repeat this verse over and over again. In his Tenth Conference he urges this method of simple and constant repetition as the best way of casting out all distractions and monkey chatter from our mind, in order for it to rest in God.[5]

Drawing on this teaching and on his experience in Malaysia, the method of meditation that John Main began to recommend was this:

> Sit down. Sit still and upright. Close your eyes lightly. Sit relaxed but alert. Silently, interiorly begin to say a single word. We recommend the prayer-word, 'Maranatha'. Recite it as four syllables of equal length. Listen to it as you say it, gently but

continuously. Do not think or imagine anything – spiritual or otherwise. If thoughts and images come, these are distractions at the time of meditation, so keep returning to simply saying the word. Meditate each morning and evening for between twenty and thirty minutes.[6]

For John Main the influence of *The Cloud* was not quite so direct as for the teachers of Centering Prayer. Yet his debt to the teaching of *The Cloud* is clear. Not only does he frequently quote from it, he gives it first place in his reading list, describing it as 'the most succinct, practical and balanced guide to meditation in the English mystical tradition'.[7]

The movement begun by John Main in 1991 became known as the World Community for Christian Meditation (WCCM). Since then it has

> spread through over a hundred countries where individuals, groups and Christian Meditation centres share the vision of peace and unity arising from meditation. Groups meet in homes, parishes, offices, hospitals, prisons and colleges. A network of Christian Meditation centres helps to serve this community and its teaching work. Dialogue with other faiths has arisen from this deepening of Christian spirituality in the lives of men and women in all walks of life. The link with the Benedictine monastic family is especially valued.[8]

Like the Centering Prayer method, the method recommended by John Main is very simple. But there is a difference of emphasis. In Centering Prayer, echoing *The Cloud*'s phrase 'naked intent unto God', the key word is 'intention', meaning a ready consent to be 'totally available' to God. The essence of this method is surrender to God's will, and 'if you catch yourself thinking, you let the thought go'.

In the discipline of Christian Meditation it is not 'intention' which is the key word so much as 'attention'. Giving full attention to the prayer word or mantra from the beginning to the end of the time set aside for meditation is the central point. The function of the prayer word is to collect and concentrate the mind, and to anchor it so that the heart can freely enter into the eternal prayer of Jesus to the Father.

When distractions arise – which is what normally happens – we return gently to the prayer word.

However, it is not only full attention that is required; it is also true that a proper intention is fundamental. It is impossible to stay present to our mantra without a strong underlying intention to do so. To sum up, while Centering Prayer puts the emphasis on the inner disposition required for the gift of contemplative prayer, Christian Meditation places it on the practice itself.

Both practices, in my understanding, are variations on *The Cloud*'s teaching of the 'one little word', the main point of difference being that the social context is totally altered. We are no longer talking about a mature practice almost entirely confined to monks and hermits, but a simple method that can be used by anyone. In its original context *The Cloud* was not intended for a spiritual beginner. A full grounding in cataphatic prayer[9] and basic moral formation was assumed. This is the revolutionary departure in both Centering Prayer and Christian Meditation.

Not surprisingly, perhaps, both movements have aroused opposition from some more traditionally formed teachers. This is because the prayer of silent meditation is only superficially simple. The technique or discipline is simple, but the theology, the psychology and the spirituality that underlie it are all subtle. Both practices require mature teaching from experienced practitioners, and psychological and spiritual support. These are regularly provided by local prayer groups, and by all possible modern means of communication – websites, CDs, DVDs, podcasts, books and oral teaching – both in English and in an increasing number of other languages. Today, contemporary teachers do not assume that beginners will have a knowledge of the Scriptures or of the contemplative tradition. But every effort is made to ensure that they are encouraged to go deeper into both the Bible and the mystical tradition as they persevere with the practice.

As we have seen from this outline of the teaching of these two movements, contemporary teachers owe much to *The Cloud of Unknowing*. But there are some areas in which its language and outlook differ significantly from current understandings of the human condition and culture. Moreover, as noted earlier, many people who have been discovering the art of contemplative prayer do not have the deep understanding or appreciation of the Church's traditional means of grace, something taken for granted by the *Cloud*-author.

Psychotherapy and stages of spiritual growth

Many present-day seekers of an authentic Christian spirituality are drawn to contemplative prayer because they feel themselves to be fragmented, and perhaps even almost overwhelmed, by the stresses and pressures of life. They are looking for healing that is holistic and addresses their deepest needs. Thomas Keating has responded to this need by linking the teaching of *The Cloud* to the insights of contemporary psychotherapy. He writes:

> Through the regular practice of contemplative prayer, the dynamism of interior purification is set in motion. This dynamism is a kind of divine psychotherapy, organically designed for each of us, to empty out our unconscious and free us from the obstacles to the free flow of grace in our minds, emotions and bodies.[10]

He states that there is now 'growing empirical evidence that traumatic emotional experiences from earliest childhood are stored in our bodies and nervous systems in the form of tension, anxiety and various defense systems'. These are not got rid of by ordinary rest and sleep; but 'in an interior silence and the profound rest that this brings to the whole organism, these emotional blocks begin to soften up and the natural capacity of the human organism to throw off things that are harmful to it starts to evacuate them'. He adds: 'Simply putting up with them, and not fighting them is the best way to release them.'

It is fair to say that Keating's teaching here is not based on *The Cloud* as such, but may in part be influenced by his reading of St John of the Cross (1542–91) as well as his knowledge of psychotherapy.

However, we can find further insights that are drawn from *The Cloud* in the teaching of both John Main and Laurence Freeman OSB, who is Main's disciple and the present Spiritual Director of WCCM. From a slightly different perspective, Main pointed out how unwilling people are to admit their deep need of healing. In a similar vein,

Freeman comments that Christian people are very ready to recognize Jesus as Lord, the triumphant captain of 'our team', or to fear him as our future judge, but less willing to admit that our personalities are seriously fragmented, torn between conflicting desires.

Laurence Freeman agrees with Angela Tilby,[11] stating that 'the need for sacramental confession, for example, has been replaced for most Westerners by the therapist'.[12] In common with contemporary teachers, he states that:

> *The Cloud*'s description of the stages of spiritual growth from the active to the highest contemplative life in a cloister has been replaced by a modern awareness of the contemplative dimension of every life style and the unique process of the complexities of individual growth.[13]

He further comments that 'reading *The Cloud* today requires us to make many necessary cultural adaptations', yet nevertheless 'it is remarkable how much of the essence of the book's tradition transmits itself directly'.

Alienation and reintegration

Nowhere is this essence of *The Cloud* more recognizable than in the process of reintegration of the human psyche. As Freeman points out, *The Cloud* makes us re-examine psychologically what we mean by individuality, and especially our understanding of who, and what, we are. Until the seventeenth century, he suggests, an individual was something or someone who could not be separated from the whole. From that time, it gradually came to mean the opposite – separated, cut off, isolated and essentially self-sufficient. We have to learn to reintegrate the two meanings, and the process of reintegration is what *The Cloud* describes. This is the ancient path of meditation.

In the experience of meditation, we eventually come up against a kind of 'brick wall', which, as Freeman says, *The Cloud* wisely prepares us for. 'Up against this barrier we discover the sorrow of our isolated individuality, our being separated individuals. But if we persevere we can break through this wall into the joy of boundless being, as individuals indivisible from the whole.'[14]

In a publication from 2007,[15] Freeman expands on this image of the psychological brick wall. Quoting *The Cloud*'s two phrases – 'the naked awareness of self' in which we experience 'the sorrow of existence'[16] – he comments:

> this sorrow is not the same as depression, it is rather the sadness we feel because the ego always prevents us from being *fully* open, *fully* present. The ego prevents us from giving ourselves totally to another person or to God. So the ego is like a ball and chain because it prevents us from running, from being really free.

The *Cloud*-author points out that there is an impasse here. On the one hand, this self-conscious awareness of oneself must go before we can enter into true contemplative prayer. On the other hand, this self-awareness cannot be got rid of by our own efforts, only by the grace given freely by God.

Present and future

Like the author of *The Cloud*, contemporary teachers have necessarily to struggle with the limitations of language when speaking of a prayer of silence that is essentially beyond all images and words. However, we now know more than the *Cloud*-author could possibly have dreamed of about the workings and structure of the human brain. It is established by clinical research, for example, that regular times of contemplative prayer make desirable changes in the shape of the brain.[17]

Further developments are being actively pursued in making the fruits of contemplative prayer better known and more accessible. In parts of Australia, there has been significant progress in teaching large numbers of children in schools to meditate, and now a growing and widespread interest is being shown elsewhere in this project, not least in Britain, through the outreach programme of the WCCM.[18] The benefits of regular meditation for recovering addicts at the eleventh step are also well known, and research in the area of mental health and sickness is being developed at the present time through the same WCCM outreach programme.[19]

Interfaith dialogue

Many of those who today come to contemplative prayer in the Christian tradition are disillusioned with the institutional Church; or they may come from a post-Christian background, or have dipped into Eastern traditions of teaching and practice. The World Community for Christian Meditation is open to dialogue with other faiths, believing that silent meditation is in its essence a universal human practice that transcends differences between the diverse faith traditions. This does not mean that contemplative prayer can be reduced to a lowest common denominator by discarding the diverse religious traditions in which it has been nurtured. Every practice has its own understanding and its own tradition behind it. Some come from a theistic tradition, in which the grace, generosity and compassion of a Supreme Being are axiomatic; others are non-theistic, stressing the human fruits of the practice.

Whatever the teaching, it is the actual practice that increasingly brings people of different traditions under one roof to pray together in silence and stillness.[20] The growth of movements in all religions that teach contemplative prayer could have the potential to become the primary driver of a new global spirit of unity within the human family.

Notes

———•◦•———

The abbreviation *CU* refers to *The Cloud of Unknowing* (ed. Spearing) and is followed by the relevant chapter number. Notes consisting of chapter numbers only refer to chapters in this book.

Foreword

1 Clifton Wolters (ed.), *The Cloud of Unknowing and Other Works* (London: Penguin, 1961), ch. 4, para. 13.

Introduction

1 *The Cloud of Unknowing*, ed. A. C. Spearing (London: Penguin, 2001), includes also *The Mystical Theology of St Denis*, *The Book of Privy Counselling* and *An Epistle on Prayer*.

2 See information and contact details at the end of this book.

1 Is contemplative prayer for me?

1 The words are closely related to the opening prayer in the traditional Eucharist of the Anglican tradition and to the Collect of the Roman Catholic Votive Mass of the Holy Spirit, although in these liturgies it is the Holy Spirit which is directly sought.

2 Archbishop of Canterbury, 1961–74; see especially his *Be Still and Know* (London: Collins, 1982).

3 *CU*, ch. 75.

4 Psalm 42.1–2.

5 *CU*, ch. 1.

6 The original word is 'lyame': the thong by which a hawk or hunting dog was held.

7 Hosea 11.1, 4.

8 John 15.16.

9 *CU*, ch. 2.

10 Chapter 8.

11 *CU*, ch. 64.

12 The opening of Augustine's *Confessions*.

13 *CU*, chs 74, 75.

14 *CU*, ch. 74.

15 *CU*, ch. 36, last sentence.

16 Chapter 4.

17 Chapter 8.

18 *CU*, ch. 75.

19 *Mother Teresa: Come Be My Light* (London: Ebury Press, 2008).

20 Psalm 37.7.

21 Isaiah 40.31.

22 Karl Rahner SJ, 'The Spirituality of the Church of the Future', *Theological Investigations*, Vol. 20 (London: Darton, Longman and Todd, 1981), pp. 149–50.

2 One little word

1 *CU*, ch. 3, first sentence.

2 *CU*, ch. 1.

3 A. C. Spearing (ed.), *The Cloud of Unknowing and Other Works* (London: Penguin, 2001), p. 145, note 10.

4 BBC Radio 4, *Today*, 30 October 2009.

5 Spearing, *The Cloud*, p. 146, note 13.

6 Matthew 5.8.

7 1 Corinthians 13.12.

8 C. K. Barrett, *A Commentary on the First Epistle to the Corinthians* (London: A & C Black, second edn, 1971), p. 306.

9 Simone Weil (1909–43) was a brilliant philosopher, political activist, theologian and mystic. Born in Alsace-Lorraine into a non-practising Jewish family, she died of TB in Ashford in Kent. For a time, she worshipped at the same church in New York as Thomas Merton before he became a monk, but there is no evidence that they ever met.

10 C. S. Lewis, *The Screwtape Letters* (London: Geoffrey Bles, 1942).

11 Chapter 6.

12 *CU*, ch. 37.

13 *CU*, ch. 1, p. 1.

14 *The Book of Privy Counselling*, ch. 1, in Spearing, *The Cloud*, p. 105.

15 Augustine, *Confessions*, III, 6, quoted by Martin Laird, *Into the Silent Land* (London: Darton, Longman and Todd, 2006), p. 8.

16 Augustine, *Confessions*, X, 27.

17 *CU*, ch. 37.

18 Sermon preached at Lancing College Chapel in 2007 at the dedication of a window commemorating Bishop Trevor Huddleston.

19 *CU*, ch. 38.

20 'I pray that you may have the power to comprehend with all the saints, what is the breadth and length and height and depth, and to know the love

of Christ which surpasses all knowledge, so that you may be filled with all the fullness of God' (Ephesians 3.17–19).

21 Romans 8.39.

3 Two clouds

1 A. C. Spearing (ed.), *The Cloud of Unknowing and Other Works* (London: Penguin, 2001).

2 The cover shows an illumination of the Trinity, from a fifteenth-century manuscript in the Fitzwilliam Museum, University of Cambridge [Ms.378 r] (photo: Bridgeman Art Library).

3 *CU*, ch. 6.

4 *CU*, ch. 6.

5 *CU*, ch. 6.

6 James Walsh SJ (*The Cloud of Unknowing*, New York: Paulist Press, 1981) renders this 'spiritual eye'. Phyllis Hodgson's original Middle English text (*The Cloud of Unknowing and The Book of Privy Counselling*, Oxford: Oxford University Press, 1944) has 'goostly iye'.

7 St Gregory of Nyssa (*c*.330–90), *The Life of Moses* (Classics of Western Spirituality, Abraham Malherbe and E. Ferguson, New York: Paulist Press, 1978), Book 1, sections 30, 43, 46.

8 Compare Hebrews 12.18–21.

9 Exodus 24.15–18ff.

10 For example 1 Corinthians 10.1–4; Galatians 4.24–31.

11 *CU*, chs 58–60.

12 *CU*, ch. 5.

13 *Benjamin Major*, 4.22 (*The Twelve Patriarchs, The Mystical Ark*, and *Book Three of the Trinity* by Richard of St Victor, translation and introduction by Grover A. Zinn, London: SPCK, 1979).

14 *The Mystical Theology of St Denis*, ch. 1.

15 *CU*, ch. 26.

16 *CU*, ch. 26.

17 Chapter 8.

18 *CU*, chs 31, 32.

19 *CU*, ch. 7.

4 Two sisters

1 Luke 10.38–42.

2 *CU*, ch. 17.

3 *CU*, ch. 18.

4 *CU*, ch. 17.

5 *CU*, ch. 16.
6 *CU*, ch. 17.
7 *CU*, ch. 19.
8 *CU*, ch. 21.
9 *CU*, ch. 16.
10 *CU*, ch. 17.
11 *CU*, ch. 21.
12 *CU*, ch. 23.
13 Matthew 6.25ff.
14 See Ulrich Luz, *The Theology of the Gospel of Matthew* (Cambridge: Cambridge University Press, 1995), ch. 3.

5 Two virtues

1 *CU*, ch. 12, last sentence.
2 *CU*, ch. 12, third paragraph.
3 Philippians 2.6–8.
4 Luke 18.9–14.
5 See Chapter 2.
6 Augustine, *Retractions*, 1 (viii) 3.
7 *CU*, ch. 13, second paragraph.
8 *CU*, ch. 14.
9 *CU*, ch. 14, third paragraph.
10 *CU*, ch. 24, first paragraph.
11 Luke 10.27; Deuteronomy 6.5; Leviticus 19.18.
12 *CU*, ch. 24, second paragraph; ch. 25.
13 *CU*, ch. 24.
14 Acts 2.44ff.
15 See Chapter 6.
16 *CU*, ch. 25, first paragraph.
17 Matthew 5.44.
18 *The Cloud* (like other medieval sources) does not distinguish between Mary of Bethany and Mary Magdalene. See John 13.23; 19.26; 19.2; 21.15–17.
19 *CU*, ch. 25, third paragraph.
20 More natural in earlier centuries than it would be for us in the twenty-first.
21 1 Corinthians 12.14–26; Ephesians 4.15–16.

6 Sin and the self

1 Angela Tilby, *The Seven Deadly Sins* (London: SPCK, 2009), ch. 1.
2 *CU*, ch. 40.

3 *CU*, ch. 36.

4 *CU*, ch. 16. The woman 'in the city, who was a sinner' (Luke 7.36) to whom
   Jesus uttered these words is not named in the Gospel. In the Middle Ages
   she was commonly identified with Mary Magdalene, the woman from whom
   Jesus cast seven devils and who repented (Luke 8.32). Mary Magdalene was
   also identified as Mary of Bethany, the sister of Martha and Lazarus. See
   Chapter 5, note 18.

5 Luke 7.47.

6 Romans 7.18ff.

7 *CU*, ch. 38. See my Chapter 2.

8 *CU*, ch. 12.

9 1 Corinthians 13.3.

10 C. K. Barrett, *A Commentary on the First Epistle to the Corinthians* (London:
   A & C Black, second edn, 1971).

11 *CU*, ch. 45, third paragraph.

12 *CU*, ch. 41, first paragraph.

13 *CU*, ch. 41, second paragraph.

14 Matthew 6.33.

15 *CU*, ch. 42.

16 *CU*, chs 43, 44.

17 *CU*, ch. 44.

18 A. C. Spearing (ed.), *The Cloud of Unknowing and Other Works* (London:
   Penguin, 2001), p. 150, note 68, my italics.

19 *CU*, ch. 44, last paragraph.

20 *CU*, ch. 68, last paragraph.

21 The apophatic tradition, or the *via negativa*, which focuses entirely on God's
   transcendence, states that God is utterly beyond the reach of human language
   and understanding. See Chapter 8, note 9.

22 That is, the sixth-century teacher now known as Pseudo-Dionysius, not the
   first-century disciple of St Paul, converted in Athens (Acts 17.34), as thought
   by medieval writers.

23 *The Mystical Theology of St Denis*, which is included in Spearing, *The
   Cloud*.

24 *CU*, ch. 54.

7 Christ and The Cloud

1 Chapter 6.

2 *CU*, ch. 1; compare John 3.16; Romans 5.8; 1 John 4.9–10; Hosea 11.1–4.

3 *CU*, ch. 54; see end of my Chapter 6.

4 Matthew 6.5–13.

5 Chapter 2.

6 Chapter 5.

7 Mark 1.35; Luke 4.42; 5.16; 6.12; 9.18, 28–29; 22.40ff.

8 Hebrews 7.26.

9 Hebrews 5.7.

10 Chapter 4.

11 Cynthia Bourgeault (*Centering Prayer and Inner Awakening*, Cambridge, MA: Cowley Publications, 2004, p. 59), also states her belief that Jesus was a contemplative.

12 Philippians 1.21–23.

13 Philippians 3.8–9.

14 2 Corinthians 5.16.

15 C. K. Barrett, *A Commentary on the Second Epistle to the Corinthians* (London: A & C Black, 1973), pp. 170–2.

16 Mark 8.31–33.

17 *CU*, ch. 1, second paragraph.

18 *CU*, chs 7, 8, 12, etc.

19 *CU*, ch. 25, third paragraph; see Romans 5.12–21.

20 For example, unlike most, if not all, current Anglican liturgies, the service of Holy Communion in the Anglican Book of Common Prayer of 1662 makes no reference to the resurrection.

21 *CU*, ch. 4, seventh–eighth paragraphs.

22 A. C. Spearing (ed.), *The Cloud of Unknowing and Other Works* (London: Penguin, 2001), p. 147, note 21.

23 Chapter 4; *CU*, ch. 16, fourth paragraph.

24 Guiges du Pont, quoted in James Walsh SJ (ed.), *The Cloud of Unknowing* (New York: Paulist Press, 1981), p. 156, note 142.

25 *CU*, chs 57–62, esp. ch. 58, fourth paragraph. For Stephen's martyrdom see Acts 7.55–60.

26 Luke 24.50–53; Acts 1.6–11.

27 2 Corinthians 12.2–4.

28 *CU*, ch. 9, 2nd paragraph.

29 *CU*, chs 30, 37.

30 *CU*, ch. 45.

31 In this respect, compare the teaching of John Main OSB, which is markedly Trinitarian. Main teaches that in practising contemplative prayer we enter into the eternal prayer of Jesus to the Father in the power of the Holy Spirit.

32 Walsh, *The Cloud*, Introduction, p. 12. Compare my Chapter 1, opening remarks.

8 Contemporary teaching and practice

1 Thomas Merton, in *Centering Prayer in Daily Life and Ministry*, ed. Gustave Reininger (New York: Continuum, 2006), p. 10.

2 Chapter 4.

3 *CU*, ch. 8, fourth paragraph.

4 John Cassian, *Conferences*, book 10, esp. section 10.

5 John Main, *Word into Silence* (London: Darton, Longman and Todd, 1980), p. 9.

6 Text from a bookmark, obtainable from Christian Meditation Resources, <www.wccm.org>.

7 Main, *Word into Silence*, p. 80.

8 From the home page of <www.wccm.org>.

9 Cataphatic prayer, or the *via positiva*, is simply the usual way of approaching God through positive words, images and analogies. Apophatic prayer (*via negativa*) is approaching the silence of God, who is ultimately beyond our mental comprehension, by reaching out beyond all words, images and analogies. See Chapter 6, note 20.

10 Thomas Keating, *Open Mind, Open Heart* (New York: Continuum, 1986), chapter 9, p. 93.

11 See Chapter 6; 'feelings . . . of guilt, or worthlessness . . . tend to be endured in silence or shared, if at all, with a therapist or counsellor' (Angela Tilby, *The Seven Deadly Sins*, London: SPCK, 2009, ch. 1).

12 Laurence Freeman, Introduction to *The Cloud of Unknowing* (Rockport, MA: Element Books, 1997), pp. 12–13.

13 Compare my own comments in Chapter 4.

14 See Freeman, Introduction to *The Cloud*, pp. 4–5.

15 Laurence Freeman, *The Inner Pilgrimage: The Journey of Meditation* (Singapore: Medio Media International, 2007).

16 *CU*, chs 43, 44.

17 See Shanida Nataraja, *The Blissful Brain: Neuroscience and Proof of the Power of Meditation* (London: Gaia, 2008).

18 Ernie Christie, *Coming Home: A Guide to Teaching Christian Meditation to Children* (London: Medio Media, 2010).

19 Called 'Meditatio', this outreach programme is aimed at sharing the fruits of meditation in dialogue with the secular approach to the problems of our time. See <www.wccmmeditatio.org>.

20 For example, 'Just This Day', on 24 November 2010, brought together hundreds of people from six different world faiths in the church of St Martin-in-the-Fields, London, to pray in silence together.

For further reading and action

The Cloud of Unknowing

The Cloud of Unknowing and Other Works, edited by A. C. Spearing, London: Penguin, 2001. A contemporary version of the text, with a useful introduction, from a mainly literary perspective.

The Cloud of Unknowing (Classics of Western Spirituality), edited by James Walsh SJ, with a Preface by Simon Tugwell OP, New York: Paulist Press, 1981. An invaluable commentary by a renowned scholar.

The Cloud of Unknowing and the Book of Privy Counselling, edited by Phyllis Hodgson, Oxford: Oxford University Press for the Early English Text Society, 1944. The standard text for those who wish to read the original Middle English.

The Cloud of Unknowing and The Book of Privy Counseling, edited by William Johnston, with a Foreword by Huston Smith, Garden City, NY: Doubleday, 1996. William Johnston, a renowned Jesuit scholar of Japanese Zen, was especially interested in the interface of Christian and Buddhist spirituality.

The Cloud of Unknowing, with an introduction by Laurence Freeman OSB, original text rendered by Evelyn Underhill, Rockport, MA: Element, 1997. A useful introduction relating *The Cloud* to contemporary teaching. Underhill was a pioneer in this field, but her version of the text is now somewhat dated.

***

Centering Prayer

Thomas Keating, *Open Mind, Open Heart: The Contemplative Dimension of the Gospel*, New York: Continuum, 1986. The first book in a trilogy by the leading teacher of Centering Prayer; it was followed by *The Mystery of Christ* and *Invitation to Love*.

Basil M. Pennington, *Centering Prayer: Renewing an Ancient Christian Prayer Form*, Garden City, NY: Doubleday, 1980. Written by a hugely influential teacher of Centering Prayer, this book has sold over one million copies.

Cynthia Bourgeault, *Centering Prayer and Inner Awakening*, Cambridge, MA: Cowley Publications, 2004. A complete guidebook for all who wish to know the practice of Centering Prayer, by a Canadian Episcopal priest who is also a retreat and conference leader and the author of a number of other books.

<www.contemplativeoutreach.org> The official website of the dominant school of the Centering Prayer movement.

Christian Meditation

John Main OSB, *Word into Silence*, London: Darton, Longman and Todd, 1980. The classic introduction to Christian Meditation by the monk who recovered this ancient tradition in our time.

Laurence Freeman OSB, *Christian Meditation: Your Daily Practice*, Montreal: Novalis, 1994. A popular booklet introducing the practice of Christian Meditation.

Laurence Freeman OSB, *Jesus the Teacher Within*, with a foreword by the Dalai Lama, London: Continuum, 2000. Described as an 'excellent guide to Jesus as a key to inner transformation' by *Spirituality and Health* magazine.

<www.wccm.org> The official website of the World Community for Christian Meditation.